Birman Cats

The Owner's Guide from Kitten to Old Age

Buying, Caring for, Grooming, Health, Training and Understanding Your Birman Cat

By Rosemary Kendall

Copyright and Trademarks

Disclaimer and Legal Notice

Photo Credit: Dianne Patten of Diannes Lady Paws Birmans

Foreword

If you have never owned a Birman cat before, you are missing out on one of the most adorable and friendly cat breeds out there.

Granted, the Birman cat is quite an unusual breed which you won't find in many homes, but they really do deserve to be "discovered" and owned by more people.

Over the past fifty years I have had the pleasure of being a professional breeder and owner of my own cattery. In this time I have specialized in many breeds such as the Persian, Maine Coon and the Birman cat.

Together with the help of the other expert Birman breeders who have contributed to this book, I hope to give you an introduction to Birmans and to their basic care, as well as some insight into life with cats in general.

If you are thinking about buying one of these cats, this book is the perfect place to start, as we will be outlining the pros and cons of buying a Birman over other breeds.

Within the pages of this book you will find answers to all of your questions about Birman cats.

Here you will learn the basics about the breed, its history, temperament, appearance and more, including tips for care, training, feeding and breeding.

Rosemary Kendall

Acknowledgments

In writing this book, I also sought tips, advice, photos, and opinions from many experts of the Birman breed.

In particular I wish to thank the following wonderful experts for going out of their way to help and contribute:

USA & CANADA

Heather Reynolds of Gryphonwood Birmans
https://sites.google.com/site/gryphonwoodbirmans/

Anastasia Sky of Skyhaven Birmans
http://www.skyhavenbirmans.com/

Charli Ann Stevens of Kittablu Birmans
http://www.kittablu.com

Marilyn Rowley of Barmar Birmans
http://www.barmar.com/

Butch and Leanne Trabuc of Kanza Katz Cattery
http://www.kanzakatz.bravehost.com/

Diane Coppola of D'Elo Birmans
http://www.delobirmans.com/

Jodi Ross of Starcrystal Birman's
http://my.athenet.net/~starcrystal

Linda Birkmann of Pussetoe Birmans
http://www.pussetoebirmans.com

Dianne Patten of Diannes Lady Paws Birmans
http://www.diannesladypawsbirmans.com/

Paula & James Watson of Bitaheaven Birmans
Email: bitaheaven@tcworks.net

Joann Lamb of Xtasy
Email: lambchp@gmail.com

Jan & Merle Shelton of Templkatz Birmans
http://www.templkatz.com/

Ellen Weber of Torielle Birmans
Email: torielle9@yahoo.com

Sylvia Foulds of Angel Eyes Birmans
http://www.angel-eyes.ca

UNITED KINGDOM

The Birman Cat Club
http://birmancatclub.co.uk/

Linda Russell of Jemley Birmans
http://jemleybirmans.webs.com/

Marcia Owen of Goldlay Birmans Burmese & Singapuras
http://www.goldlay-cats.co.uk

Claire Finch of Snowwitch Birmans

Carole Morbey of Wyebrook Birman's

Ann Mott of Jandouglen Birmans
http://www.ann.mott.freeuk.com/

Acknowledgments

Caroline Lamb of Ingamae Birmans
Email: carolinelamb@ymail.com

Christina Dyer of Snowqueen Birmans
Email: cmd.318@icloud.com

Mark & Susie Harris of Mentobe Birmans
http://www.mentobecats.weebly.com

Dawn Brown of Dalteema Birmans
http://www.dalteema.co.uk/

Margaret Wignall of Bijoubirmon Birmans
http://www.bijoubirmon.co.uk/

Photo Credit: Ellen Weber of Torielle Birmans

Table of Contents

Table of Contents

Table of Contents

Chapter 1 - The World of the Birman

Welcome to a very special journey — owning a Birman cat is a life-changing event. Once you have owned one of these very special cats, your life will never be the same again.

Physically they are absolutely beautiful. A stunning silky coat is made for stroking and cuddling. The notable feature is the striking white paws, like they are wearing expensive gloves! To top it all, those piercing blue eyes like a feline version of Paul Newman.

I'm a big fan of their soft and gentle personality; showing none of the extremes I've experienced with other breeds, they tend to strike a nice middle-ground balance in most areas.

Photo Credit: Jodi Ross of Starcrystal Birman's

For example, they seek affection and love but are not overly clingy so that you are unable to do the chores or work from home without a sad face looking up at you 24-7. They will, however, definitely follow you from room to room, but without being a nuisance.

When they want attention they make it obvious in a polite way, usually with a soft meow or a fixed stare that demands you take notice.

A nice session of stroking on your lap will usually keep them going for a good while until they make it obvious again! They certainly make for a great companion cat and they will keep you de-stressed with these regular breaks being a great source of calming energies.

They really are intelligent, fiercely loyal and devoted pets. With some breeds I've owned, like the Persian, I've sometimes wanted a little more activity, but the Birman are a lot more active without being overly so. I definitely do not want a missile of fur running up and down my curtains at all hours.

On the food front, they are a pleasure, easy-going and not at all fussy, unlike some other breeds.

I think this simple unstressed nature helps them live a long and usually healthy life. I would expect most Birmans on average to live until they are 15 and I've known some friends have them live as long as 20 years in good health throughout.

The Birman is a very social pet and I would strongly advise you don't buy one if you are out at work most of the day. It isn't really fair. They will get lonely. Do at least consider getting them a companion, ideally another Birman, but to be honest any breed of cat or dog will do. They will appreciate having a friend.

As you can no doubt tell, I am a big fan of this breed. Before I get too 'carried away' let's find out about the history of the breed.

Brief History of the Birman Breed

Known as the "Sacred Cat of Burma," the exact origins of the
Birman are not precisely known but a fascinating legend has
been passed down through time. It may be a myth, or maybe
not? I certainly like to think, when looking at my Birmans, that
there must be some truth in the story!

In the Temple of Lao-Tsun on Mount Lugh in Northern Burma
lived a famous priest (known as a Lama) named Kittah Mun-Ha
who served the Goddess Tsun Kyan-Kse.

One night the temple was attacked and Mun-Ha was fatally
wounded, but before he died, his faithful companion, a cat called
Sinh, placed its paws on his master while facing a statue of the
Goddess.

A miracle occurred as the all-white cat transformed color. Sinh's
yellow eyes became a sapphire blue while his ears, nose, legs and
tail darkened to the color of the earth—with the notable
exception of his paws, which remained a pure white. His body
had a golden glow.

The other priests watched the transformation and were inspired
to fend off the raiders. By morning, all of the other cats in the
temple had the same golden fur and pure white feet.

Seven days later, Sinh died, taking the soul of Mun-Ha to
paradise. The legend states that each Sacred Cat that dies carries
the soul of a priest on its final journey to paradise.

What we do know is that the Birman did originate from Burma
and that the cat was kept and regarded as a sacred companion to
the priests in the temples.

In 1919 a pair of Birmans were sent as a reward from priests in Burma to two Englishmen living in France, Major Gordon Russell and Mr. August Pavie. Sadly, Madalpour, the male, died on the voyage to France, but Sita, the pregnant female, survived, producing kittens. One of the female kittens, Poupee, was bred to another breed, thought to probably be a Siamese, to preserve the breed.

The Birman breed was officially recognized in France in 1925 although the breed almost disappeared after World War II when records show only one male and female remaining. This pair, named Orloff and Xenia de Kaabaa, had four kittens (Manou, Lon Saito, Sjaipour, Sita 1 and Sita 2), which formed the foundation for the breed's comeback after the war. Although it was necessary to outcross to other longhaired breeds, including Persians and Siamese, the breed was saved.

In 1965 Mrs. Elsie Fisher of the Praha cattery and Mrs. Margaret Richards of Paranjoti cattery imported three cats into the UK from France, with many of today's pedigreed winners in the United Kingdom originating from these cats. The Governing Council of the Cat Fancy (GCCF) in the UK recognized the Birman as a distinct breed in 1966.

We know that the first recording of a Birman in the USA was in 1959, imported by Dr. and Mrs. John Seipel. You may also come across the legendary name of Mrs. Gertrude Griswold of Tacoma, Washington, who received two Birman cats in 1961. Her cattery, Clover Creek, was renamed as Griswold and one of her cats, Korrigan, sired the CFA's first Birman grand champion, Griswold's Romar of Bybee.

The U.S. Cat Fancier's Association (CFA) recognized the breed in 1967.

Physical Characteristics

Of course no two Birman cats will look exactly alike, but we can describe the desired look as defined by the Cat Fanciers' Association (CFA), which is the world's largest registry of pedigreed cats. This does matter if you intend to show your Birman in CFA shows but otherwise it really doesn't matter. Each Birman will have its own delightful personality regardless of looks—just like us humans!

Photo Credit: Butch & Leanne Trabuc of Kanza Katz Cattery

Head

The skull should be strong, broad, and rounded with a slight flat spot just in front of each ear and a slight flat spot on the slightly sloping backwards forehead in between the ears.

The Birman should have heavy jaws with a strong, well-developed chin with the lower jaw forming a perpendicular line with the upper lip.

The Roman nose (slightly convex shaped) should be medium length and width. The nostrils are set low on the nose leather.

Cheeks are full with a rounded muzzle which should be neither short and blunted nor pointed and narrow. The fur is short in appearance about the face, but longer to the extreme outer area of the cheek.

Eyes

Birmans have striking sapphire blue eyes which are shaped almost round and of a relatively large size and set well apart, giving the face a sweet expression with the outer corner tilted slightly upward. Very few Birmans have round, Persian-type eyes.

Ears

Medium-sized ears with good width between them. Almost as wide at the base as tall. Modified to a rounded point at the tip and set as much to the side as into the top of the head.

Body

This medium to large pedigree cat has a solid and strong build with an average weight of 8 – 12 lbs. / 3.63 – 5.44 kg. Males are usually slightly larger than females. I've noticed they are longer in the body than my Persians and have longer tails and nose. The Birman should have substantial boning and be stockily built.

Legs should be heavy and medium in length with large round firm paws with five toes in front and four behind. The tail should be medium in length.

Kittens only become fully grown in their third year.

Coat

The coat is of medium length and silky, although not as thick as a Persian cat and requiring a lot less maintenance, as they do not have an undercoat.

There should be a heavy ruff around the neck and slightly curly on stomach. Because it won't mat as much, a little combing every so often will suffice, rather than daily grooming as required with a Persian. Fortunately for those who don't like vacuuming, they don't shed much and this can be reduced further by proper nutrition and regular grooming.

The Birman is sometimes confused by people thinking they are other breeds, most commonly the Siamese and Himalayan (which is actually a color-pointed Persian) breeds—this occurs due to similarities in coat colors between these cats and the Birman.

Colors

The Birman has a white to cream coat color with colored points and the four distinctive white feet (gloves). Popular point colors are Seal (dark brown), Blue (slate gray), followed by Lilac and Chocolate.

Newer colors and patterns include Red and Cream points, as well as Tabby, Tortie, and Tortie-Tabby points. All of these colors can be either the traditional solid pattern or the dramatic lynx (striped) pattern. With age, the coat develops a "golden mist" of shading, which is more apparent in Seal points.

Note – CFA changed the term lynx to tabby in 2014 because the rest of the world, including Europe and Asia, call them tabbies.

Gloves & Laces

You will know a Birman because the feet are always pure white. When they are born they are all white, but within a few days they start to color as if they are going to be seal points; the points then appear in around a week for the darker colors and two weeks for the lighter or "clear" points.

Seal point is a type of coloration where a cat has a pale body and relatively darker extremities, i.e. the face, ears, feet, and tail.

The white on the feet and up the back of the hocks (known as gloves and laces) will begin to appear within a few days on darker colors, sometimes taking several weeks to appear on the lighter colors.

The amount of white on the feet is a deciding factor in whether a Birman is eligible to be entered into cat shows.

The Birman walks with confidence, head held high with an expressive gaze on their broad face.

Indoor or Outdoor Pets?

Although I appreciate that this is very much a personal choice, I will say that I have taken the decision not to allow my cats to go outside. This is down to a number of factors such as the Birman being an expensive pedigreed cat and a long-haired one at that, requiring a minimum amount of grooming without getting all dirty and muddy!

Then there is the common sense reasoning that a cat allowed outdoors is prone to vastly increased risks of catching fleas, worms and disease, as well as possible injury from fighting with other animals, to the obvious consideration of dangerous road traffic. There is also the risk of theft.

Call it selfish if you will, but I love my Birmans so much that I want them to enjoy living as long as possible and I don't believe they are deprived at all by not being allowed access to the outside world and its many dangers.

Should I Buy One or Two?

Two or more Birmans will get along well in a household, especially if you buy them at the same time and age—adopting them from the same litter is obviously best. On average a litter will be 2-4 kittens.

Although you will be responsible for the regular combing of two cats, the Birman is a lot less effort than some other long-haired breeds, so this needn't be seen as such a drawback.

The main decision really comes down to the costs of buying a Birman, which admittedly can be considerable, and the ongoing costs. If possible, I would certainly encourage you to consider buying two, as they are great at keeping each other company, especially during the inevitable times when you need to be out of the house.

Is a Birman Suitable for a Family?

All in all, I have found Birmans to be fine family cats, generally performing more of an observational role than a participatory one. If he doesn't like what's going on, he simply removes himself rather quickly. It is really a case of teaching your children to be gentle and respectful with any animal.

Any cat, no matter how gentle and well behaved, will react if it is being handled roughly or harassed. That's simply in the animal's nature. In those situations, I honestly think it is the child that needs to be instructed in better behavior, rather than the cat.

Photo Credit: Charli Ann Stevens of Kittablu Birmans

Which is Best – Male or Female?

This is a question that always seems to come up, and in my opinion it really comes down to a personal preference, as I have not noticed a lot of difference in the personality and temperament between males and females.

All cats, regardless of gender, are individuals. They all have distinct personalities, and they all respond to their life experiences. I have had many cats of all species and both genders, including Birmans. They are all lovely, well-mannered, sweet pets no matter the gender.

Both male and female Birmans are like most cats—couch potatoes, so once the males are altered, this is even more the case. I suppose if I were put on the spot I would say the female

Birmans are more independent and males are more likely to be lap cats, in my experience.

Kitten or Adult?

Heather Reynolds of Gryphonwood Birmans has some advice:

"In North America it is common for cats that have finished their show and breeding careers to be retired into pet homes where they get to live out the rest of their lives as the King or Queen of their new home. A retiree can make a wonderful pet for those people who wish to avoid the trials of kittenhood. Retirees have often been intensely socialized for the rigors of showing and travelling and ideally represent the best health, temperament and physical conformation as breeding cats."

Birmans and Other Pets

Although we humans like to think of a cat as a solitary animal, quite happy being left to get on with things, I've always found the Birman cat does suffer from loneliness and shouldn't be left alone for long periods of time. Because of this trait it is a positive advantage to have other pets, including dogs.

One thing worth pointing out is that Birmans can be quite dominant when placed beside other breeds; you'll definitely have your Birman thinking he's in charge of the household!

Grooming Requirements

Although a longhaired breed, the Birman does not need the kind of constant grooming required by other heavily coated cats like the Persian. Perhaps because the Birman does have "forest cat" blood, their silky fur resists tangling and can be well managed with regular combing. They benefit from periodic baths including degreasing.

I'll discuss this more fully in the chapter on daily care, but oddly enough, Birmans do not necessarily shed more than any other breed of cat. They will experience periods of seasonal shedding as the warm months are coming on, but for all their luxuriant appearance, the degree to which they shed is much more an individual characteristic than an overall breed trait.

Do Males Spray?

Spraying can happen with a male cat of any breed, but it is not an issue with which I've ever had to deal, even with my intact males. In neutered male Birmans, spraying is highly unlikely for the simple reason that they are typically altered within the first six months of life. At that age, they're too young to have even contemplated the spraying behavior.

Many people do not realize that female cats can spray too, but again, this is extremely rare behavior. In my experience, cats that are happy, healthy, and well cared for just don't spray. This is a stereotype that is unfairly applied to toms, and in my experience indicative of an unhappy or physically ill cat.

If spraying does occur, it is much more typical in a multi-cat household where issues of territoriality arise. Again, however, this is not an issue I've faced with my cats, even when I've had 25 and more at one time.

Advantages and Disadvantages

I have never been all that comfortable with putting together a list of pros and cons for any type of animal, much less for any specific breed within the species. Here's why.

I love dogs. I was raised with Yorkshire Terriers and love their feisty dispositions and determined way of being in the world, but I have absolutely no desire to own a dog for the simple reason that I don't want to have to walk one. Another person might say that's the *best* reason to have a dog. My "con" is their "pro."

For me, changing a litter box is just a mindless chore, not pleasant or unpleasant, just something that has to be done. Other people think it's the worst job imaginable. Those folks don't need to be keeping a cat of any breed.

I think Birmans are incredible cats, they are devoted, loyal and highly intelligent. Here are just some brief pros and cons:

Pros

• Gentle in nature and unstressed—they lead a long life on average.

• Beautiful and with a unique look that makes them stand out from the cat crowd.

• A great companion, involving itself in your life and keen on receiving reciprocal love and affection.

• They are not loud or overly active – an ideal temperament.

• Not known to have obvious health defects.

• Low maintenance in terms of grooming.

Cons

• They are pedigreed and therefore expensive compared to most other breeds.

• Best kept indoors, so more changing and cleaning of the litter tray than cats allowed outdoors.

• Can suffer from loneliness. Best not left alone for long periods.

We asked Diane Coppola of D'Elo Birmans why she believes potential new owners consider the Birman compared to other breeds of cat.

"The Birman is a great cat for just about anyone, they are easy going, beautiful, with their sparkling blue eyes and distinctive white feet, they get along well with children, dogs and other cats. If you want a happy, healthy, middle of the road cat who wants to be your best friend but understands when you are busy and can give you some alone time, the Birman is a good choice. They love to be groomed but are very low maintenance in spite of their semi long hair, which generally does not mat. Once you have one you will want more!!!!"

Jodi Ross of Starcrystal Birman's says this:

"Birmans are quite intelligent... I can teach them many things such as fetching, going up for a treat and doing agility where they go through tunnels, hoops, etc. This is what makes them the most dog-like breed. They will typically come to their name as well and can learn responses to your words, like dogs."

Chapter 2 - Choosing a Birman Breeder

Before we get too involved in the detail of finding and choosing a Birman breeder, let's look at exactly what it means to adopt a cat that has a registered pedigree.

To be certain that you are adopting a purebred Birman cat, you should locate a cattery that specializes only in this breed and purchase a kitten with a traceable "family tree" history.

As proof of the legitimacy of their bloodlines, a good cattery will join one or more of the major cat registries. This reassures new customers of the authenticity of their breed claims.

Photo Credit: Jodi Ross of Starcrystal Birman's

The best-known and largest of the cat registries are the Cat Fanciers' Association (CFA), The International Cat Association (TICA), The American Cat Fanciers' Association (ACFA), and for the UK the Governing Council of the Cat Fancy (GCCF):

http://www.cfa.org
http://www.tica.org
http://www.acfacat.com/
http://www.gccfcats.org

Clearly this is not the only path for buying a Birman cat, but by working with a cattery where the animals have registered pedigrees, you will be seeing the finest examples of the breed.

The additional benefit of adopting a kitten produced from verifiable bloodlines is that it is actively cultivated to avoid potential genetic health problems. Although the initial price can often appear "expensive," the absence of health problems can save you a small fortune in vet fees.

Pedigreed cats can be registered with cat associations because they are qualified examples of their type and they will "breed true." This means that if you mate a Birman male with a Birman female, the kittens will have the same physical traits as the parents.

Breeders work toward achieving the points of the recognized "breed standard" for the cats they raise. This list of accepted requirements is used as the basis for judging in cat shows.

Pedigreed Birman cats aren't fashion accessories and shouldn't be adopted on a whim. You should know the breed, and value it for its specific and special qualities. In doing so, and in working with qualified and reputable breeders, you are supporting the continued cultivation of the cats according to the accepted standard of excellence rather than supporting the "kitten mills."

Pet-Quality Birmans

Buying a purebred Birman cat can be expensive - but you don't need to go to the lengths of buying a show-quality Birman. "Pet quality" Birman kittens are not "sub-standard." They simply don't conform precisely enough to the recognized breed standard to be entered in shows or used in breeding programs.

In all honesty, most people can't tell the difference between pet and show Birman cats. Sometimes just the markings on the feet can make the difference between a pet and a top show cat. For most people, the reasons will probably be too minor to even be detected and are nothing to do with health. Certainly the "so-called flaw" won't be consequential enough to be an adoption "deal breaker." Pet-quality kittens are beautiful animals with excellent pedigrees.

The photo above is an example of the very small differences in foot markings that make a pet- versus show-quality Birman. This is Gryphonwood Leo showing off his seal point colored toes.

If you are buying a Birman kitten as "pet-quality," often they will have already been spayed or neutered by the breeder. This ensures the continuity of the cattery's bloodlines and prevents undesirable traits from being passed on.

Very often the difference is much more subtle. There is a one hundred point standard for the perfect Birman. Points are assigned for each trait such as shape of the head, chin, muzzle, ear size and placement, eyes (shape, color, and placement), body size and condition, color, and markings. A cat with perfect markings may be a pet because his ears are too tall. Or perhaps his nose doesn't have the characteristic roundness. Pet quality is never determined by health.

How Catteries Operate

Buying a Birman kitten is not as simple as turning up at a cattery, putting your money on the table and walking away with a kitten.

Birman breeders dedicate a major portion of their lives to caring for their cats and selectively honing their cattery's bloodlines to create premier representatives of the breed.

They are passionate about their cats and they usually have long waiting lists. They certainly don't have to sell you one, unless they are absolutely sure their kittens are going to a good home.

You can certainly expect a breeder to have a long list of questions for you to ensure your suitability as a parent for their babies. Any breeder showing anything less than this commitment should be taken extremely cautiously. A "cattery" that allows you to walk in and leave with a cat is likely to be a kitten mill. Be wary of catteries that offer to ship to you without meeting you.

No true cat lover wants to support that kind of operation.

I've definitely turned prospective purchases away because I wasn't comfortable with my gut feeling and I've had to put the cat's interests first. I always ask any potential "parent" if they have previous experience with cats, and if so, what kind. I listen to how the person responds. I like people who ask lots of questions and are clearly trying to learn everything about the breed from the onset of the relationship.

In return I will definitely be expecting to answer a series of questions and be able to provide references from former clients. A breeder who will not provide references to you would, in my opinion, not be someone you'd want to deal with.

Linda Birkmann of Pussetoe Birmans offers an insight into how breeders operate: "My cats are part of our family and are in our home, as with most North American breeders. Unlike dogs, for the most part we do not have facilities to tour. Kittens are raised with their mothers in our bedroom when they are very young. They are then moved to a spare bedroom that has been kitten proofed for their socialization phase.

I keep the moms with the kittens when people come to see kittens in the kitten room. I will bring out the dad and allow them to meet prospective people. The older cats I have running freely in my house, everyone is welcome to pet. Visitors are not allowed in with new moms and babies, and this is a function of the youngsters not having fully developed immune systems. I do not care to expose them until they are 8+ weeks."

Finding and Evaluating Reputable Breeders

I would definitely recommend familiarizing yourself with the breed by attending cat shows, where you will be able to make contact with professional breeders from your area.

We will discuss showing your Birman cat later, but even if that is not your intention, these cat shows are a wonderful opportunity to see beautiful examples of the breed and to meet breeders face to face.

This certainly isn't the place to purchase a Birman because breeders will be preoccupied with showing their cats, but you can definitely get business cards and "get a feeling" for people that you are comfortable dealing with in the future. Take the opportunity to ask about upcoming litters and whether you can get on the waiting list.

Follow up by asking some more in-depth questions at a later date by telephone, and once you feel comfortable about potentially preceding, you can organize an appointment at the cattery.

Information You Want from the Breeder

Be prepared for your first visit to a cattery. You'll forget how to speak English and will spend a lot of time cooing and saying, "Awwwwwww!!!"

You should have all of your questions prepared in advance, including some of the following points.

- How long has the cattery been established?
- How big is the operation?
- Do they work with breeds other than the Birman? Now or in the past?
- With what associations are the kittens registered?
- How much support down the road is there if problems arise?
- Is there pet insurance?

- How long have you been breeding?
- Does the breeder exhibit the animals in organized cat shows? Why or why not?

Beware of dealing with any breeder who, when presented with these and similar questions:

- Is vague or evasive with their responses and seems to lack a basic knowledge of the breed.
- Denies that potential genetic issues are associated with the breed or assures you that all such problems have been completed eradicated from their cats.
- Doesn't seem to be actively involved with the cats.
- Refuses to let you tour the cattery or to interact with the cats.
- Can't produce documentation of health screenings and ancestry.
- Brushes off the need for all cats to be properly socialized before adoption.

Ask about both the kitten's parents:

- Are they healthy?
- How many litters has the female delivered?
- Have all of her kittens from past litters been healthy?
- Who is the father?
- Have the two cats produced litters together in the past?
- Why have these cats been chosen as a breeding pair?

You should be allowed to see the health records for both cats. Examine the information carefully. Make sure the cats have seen a veterinarian on a routine basis and have received their vaccinations.

If other tests and procedures are listed, find out why they were required. Make note of words or phrases you don't understand and either look them up online or discuss them with your own vet.

Charli Ann Stevens of Kittablu Birmans adds: "In many cases breeders do their own vaccinations, so they may not have official vet records on their cats. Personally, I take my kittens to the veterinarian to have that for the kitten buyer. However, the adults are managed at home. Also, with the changing thoughts on vaccinating cats, many people may find that following the first few years of shots, many veterinarians are changing their minds on annual vaccines for cats (except of course rabies) due to the issue with sarcomas—especially if the cats are indoor only cats."

If possible, meet and interact with the parents. Their personalities are not necessarily a measurement of the kitten's nature, but I've found it to be a pretty good indicator, especially in a breed as sweet natured as the Birman.

- What kind of health care did the female receive during her pregnancy?
- How did the delivery go?
- Was it a normal birth?
- Were the kittens able to nurse without problems?
- Have they needed any special health care?
- Have they ever been treated for fleas or worms?
- Have they received their first vaccination?
- When are the boosters due?
- Will you receive copies of all the health records?

Always make certain that you understand any type of health guarantee that is included in the adoption agreement and what if anything you have to do, like have the baby evaluated by a veterinarian, to ensure the guarantee is not voided.

Photo Credit: Charli Ann Stevens of Kittablu Birmans

Birman Names

Of course, you can name your new Birman cat anything you like no matter how crazy it sounds. Something, however, you may find curious when visiting breeders is the tradition that many breeders follow. This derives from France, where kittens born in a certain year are given names beginning with the designated letter of the alphabet for that year. Each year the next letter of the alphabet will be used until the cycle of 26 letters begins again with the letter A.

Socialization Methods

It's especially important to discuss socialization with the breeder. Most kittens are not made available for adoption until they have reached 3 months of age. By then, they should be litter box trained and familiar with a scratching post in addition to having been weaned.

The best Birman breeders will make sure that their kittens are handled on a daily basis and given plenty of opportunity to interact with other cats of all ages.

This period of socialization is incredibly important to their future well-being. All of this intellectual stimulation is essential to keep those bright, curious little minds happy. A bored kitten is trouble on four paws!

The Birman kittens should also have reasonable exposure to normal household and environmental circumstances. Eleven years ago I adopted two Russian Blues from the same litter, who had been in foster care for 11 months.

They were and are lovely cats, but they had hardly ever seen another human being. The woman who cared for them admitted she had no friends. After all these years with me, my boys still do a disappearing act when people visit our home.

When cats are exposed to noises, other animals, children, and just life in general at a young age, they are less reactive and anxious as adults. Just because Birmans are naturally well adjusted does not eliminate the need for this early socialization.

Handling Kittens

When you actually get to meet and play with the Birman kittens, be prepared to be asked to use hand sanitizer. This is a good sign that you are working with a knowledgeable breeder.

This isn't for your benefit, it is to protect the kittens because many feline diseases are highly communicable and stringent sanitation precautions are necessary.

The first time you hold a baby Birman, you'll be absolutely

floored by their sweetness and what soft, fluffy little fur balls they are. Still, you should be paying attention to some particulars about the kitten's condition—before you're cooing baby talk and picking out names.

- The coat should be lusciously soft and completely intact with no bald spots or matting. The kitten should smell and feel clean.

- Get a look at the kitten's skin by gently blowing on the fur to create a part. There should be no visible flakiness that would indicate dry skin.

- Look for fur that is soft, shiny, and completely intact with no bald patches.

- Ask the breeder to gently pull back the baby's lips so you can see the gums, which should be pink and healthy looking.

- Gently turn the kitten over on its back and have a look at the "armpits" and under the tail to look for black gravel-like specks called "flea dirt."

I recommend seeing both parents of the new kitten. Temperament does breed through genetically, and if either parent is bad tempered or unfriendly it is not advisable to purchase the kittens. It is a risk not worth taking, in my opinion.

Don't panic if the kittens have a flea or two—that really is relatively normal and you shouldn't think it's a deal breaker or decide on the spot that the cattery is poorly run. Fleas are the plague of every breeder's existence. It's far too easy for them to hitch a ride indoors on someone's pants leg and then the fight is on. This is especially true in areas where the climate is warm year round.

Having said that, you certainly want to be wary of a kitten that is overrun with fleas. In truly severe infestations fleas can be responsible for sufficient blood loss to cause anemia. If fleas are present, you want to make sure they're taken care of before you bring the kitten to your own home.

Call me old-fashioned but I am categorically against all forms of chemical flea control, no matter how "safe" they are supposed to be. Ask the breeder to bathe the kitten prior to adoption. When you get home, immediately start using a fine-tooth flea comb to snag any survivors.

The fleas get caught in the tines of the comb, which you can submerge in a glass of hot, soapy water to kill the parasites. Wash all the kitten's bedding on a daily basis for a week or two to ensure that no flea eggs are allowed to hatch.

Admittedly some of the breeders involved in the book did believe that chemical spot treatments are safe and not harmful, so do make your own decision on this issue.

Charli Ann Stevens of Kittablu Birmans says: "In discussing flea treatments, Capstar(R) really should be mentioned. The product kills 99% of adult fleas within 30 minutes. Thus, the fleas do not have time to get a blood meal or lay eggs before they die. This is huge because it eliminates the need for attempting to bomb (which doesn't work) and the need for the topical skin applications. On the downside, it only lasts about 36 hours."

- The kitten's eyes should be slightly oval in shape with a sweet and innocent expression that is also bright, curious, and very interested. Make sure there is no evidence of any kind of runny discharge.

- Examine the area around the nostrils. They should be equally free of discharge with no dry encrusted mucous.

The kitten's body should already feel solid, with a good padding of healthy fat over the ribs. You should be able to lightly feel the ribs, but the little cat should be neither emaciated nor obese.

Photo Credit: Mark & Susie Harris of Mentobe Birmans

Signing the Adoption Contract

Kittens should not be offered for adoption before 12 weeks of age. When both parties are agreed on the adoption, you will be asked to sign a written contract. All catteries have their own adoption agreements, but standard features of the document will include the following.

It is common for the contract to contain a stipulation that within 5 days a qualified veterinarian should evaluate the kitten's health. You will also be asked to provide written documentation of your compliance with this provision. This establishes a baseline measure of the kitten's condition in case the health guarantee has to be invoked.

Strict Prohibitions Against Declawing

Unless the adoption agreement you sign includes strong and pointed language against the inhumane practice of declawing cats, I would be extremely suspicious of the cattery with which you are dealing.

This hideous practice is illegal in Europe, and in many parts of the United States, as well it should be. The benign term "declawing" masks the gruesome fact that the procedure necessitates the amputation of the last digit of each of the cat's toes. It is terribly painful and negatively affects the animal's mobility for life while depriving the cat of its primary means of self-defense.

Birmans are no more or less prone to scratching than any other kind of cat, but any cat can be trained to behave appropriately with its claws if provided with the proper apparatus early in life.

I will always maintain the only "justification" for the radical surgical removal of the claws is convenience for the owner. It is not a move designed to support the wellbeing of the cat. And yes, I am extremely passionate about this topic and rightly so.

Basic Terms of the Adoption Agreement

In the papers to complete the adoption of a pedigreed Birman, you should see all the following basic provisions and terms:

- The agreed upon price.
- The gender of the kitten and a stipulation about spaying or neutering (this may have been done already by the breeder).

- Any other stipulations regarding the final release of the registration papers.
- The registered names of the breeding pair.
- A description of the specific cat being adopted, including the correct terminology for coat color and pattern if present.
- Complete contact information for both parties entering into the agreement.

Other provisions could include any of the following:

- A promise to provide ongoing health care via the services of a qualified veterinarian, including the administration of recommended vaccinations.
- Stipulation that you understand the grooming requirements of the Birman breed along with an assurance that those requirements will be routinely and appropriately met.
- A promise to contact the breeder should it become necessary for you to give up the cat rather than sell the animal to a third party or surrender it to a shelter.

It's extremely important that you understand that last point. No breeder wants to see one of their cats in a bad living situation or given over to a rescue organization where its fate will either be uncertain, or where it could be euthanized as an unwanted animal.

I cannot emphasize this strongly enough. In the event that you must give up a pedigreed animal, *contact the breeder*. I will always take back one of my cats and either keep the animal or find a way to place it in a new home.

In such a situation, however, I do require that the cat be tested for FELV/FIV, fecal parasites, and ringworm before it comes into my possession. These measures are meant to safeguard my other cats before reintroducing the individual into the population.

Rescue Groups

Before you consider contacting breeders of Birman kittens, why not do some searching for rescue cats? It does seem hard to believe, but there are plenty of owners out there who tire of the requirements and hard work necessary in owning a pet cat.

Unfortunately, people who think they know what is really involved in having a cat purchase pedigreed animals, including Birmans, with the best of intentions, and then find that they're in over their heads.

Longhaired cats can be the ones to suffer the most because they are not low maintenance pets. Birmans are easier than other breeds like Persians, which can be a constant combing and brushing project, but their coats still need attention.

Even with the concerted efforts of breeders to make sure animals are returned to them, pedigreed cats—in fact cats of all kinds— are turned over to shelters every day.

In other instances the animals are left alone in the world when their elderly owners die. Pets also suffer economic hardship when families fall on hard times and can no longer afford to care for them.

Even if you do not go this route to acquire your cat, consider supporting the efforts of local no-kill shelters either with your donations or by volunteering. Animal shelters are always in desperate need of funds, supplies, and helping hands.

People who work with and on behalf of homeless pets perform a vital service in the cause for animal welfare in the world. They are also some of the kindest and most generous folks you will ever meet. Please find a way to help them do what they do so selflessly and with such dedication.

Photo Credit: Caroline Lamb of Ingamae Birmans

Cost of Buying a Birman

There are many factors which affect the price of a Birman, including the availability in a given area and the quality of the cattery's bloodlines. Although it's a very broad range to throw out, you should expect to pay anywhere from $650–$1200+ for a pet-quality kitten and $1500 and up for a show-quality animal. (When you start considering show animals, the prices are typically much higher.)

In the United Kingdom the price of a pet Birman cat with accredited breeders is now £475 to £1000.

If you cannot afford these prices then consider a Birman rescue or a retired breeding cat. Breeders retire their cats from the breeding program to incorporate new lines, give the cat a chance to live as a pet, the queen is getting too old to continue breeding, the cats are passing along problems, etc. The retired cats usually cost substantially less money than a kitten.

Beware of kittens offered at really low prices with the claim that they are pedigreed Birmans; this is an immediate red flag alert and you could find yourself inadvertently helping to support the unconscionable activities of what are known as kitten mills. It's one thing to find someone offering Birman kittens for adoption because they just had a litter and cannot keep them all, and another to encounter a "cattery" with a constant supply of low-priced kittens for sale.

Be very suspicious of breeders who tell you to "check back in a few weeks." Reputable catteries only allow their females to deliver litters once or twice per year to minimize the physical stress for the mother. At almost any cattery, you are much more likely to have your name placed on a waiting list than immediately purchase a kitten. A red flag would be a breeder with a very large number of cats and kittens, all caged.

Be very wary of catteries that are not interested in meeting you in person and that will quite happily ship a Birman kitten to you regardless of where you live in the world. Serious breeders will always want to meet you and ensure that their cats are going to a good home.

Considering Becoming a Birman Breeder?

As a former professional breeder myself, I would heartily encourage you to not consider breeding your Birman cats. So the reason to include this section is because I want to show you just how much hard work goes into breeding in the hope that I will put you off!

While I appreciate that every successful breeder out there had to start as a virtual beginner in the first place, I just want you to realize how much commitment, money and time goes into the process so that you will consider it very seriously. Too many people become what we call backyard breeders.

There are entire books devoted to the mechanics of becoming a professional cat breeder. That discussion isn't my purpose here, but I do have a few observations I'd like to share.

When I sit down with a prospective breeder, I have to smother a laugh when they tell me they expect to open a cattery as a profitable business.

Yes, purebred Birman kittens, or any other breed for that matter, on the face of it do seem to cost a lot of money, but when you become a breeder you realize just how high the expenses are.

The best breeders of pedigreed cats are those that do it for the love of the breed, demonstrating a passion, love and a determination to adhere to strict breed standards.

It should be mentioned that not all catteries (unlike most other types of animal breeders) offer stud service. Many catteries are closed and do not offer stud service. Although even within many closed catteries, there may be exceptions to that rule. It's not like a horse or a cow or dog, where stud service is available to about anyone agreeing to the contract for the stud service.

Obstacles and Downsides

If you like your life to be a comfortable routine, then breeding Birman cats will turn it upside down. Get ready to be on standby at all hours of the day—and night. Often at the most unexpected times you will find yourself having to nurse a sick kitten or deal with an emergency that you most probably have not foreseen. You will certainly find it very hard to be able to go away for short breaks and vacations, so to a large extent you are going to be tied down to your cattery.

It is very hard to be businesslike and calm and collected when you have to say goodbye to your kittens, which inevitably you have become rather attached to!

It's also heartbreaking dealing with the young kittens that unfortunately died early on either in birth or soon afterwards.

A sizeable amount of capital will be required to start your breeding business. Initially you will need foundation animals for your line or the stud fees if you can't afford to buy a breeding pair.

Then all sorts of equipment will be required, as well as ongoing costs such as food, supplies and veterinary expenses. The medical expenses alone can quickly wipe out any profits, especially if your cats become sick and need medicine or operations.

Do you know if you are even allowed to run a business from home? Perhaps you need a permit or license? With plenty of potential clients visiting your home you may find that neighbors may start to become resentful of issues such as noise and parking.

It could also be that your home insurance policy may be invalid if you are running a business.

If you are a member of a homeowner's association then you may find out that HOA rules and regulations restrict your ability to have above a certain amount of cats?

You will also certainly need to look into legislation for your individual state, as some require you to commit to yearly inspections by the Department of Agriculture.

Reality Check

Rereading this section I have got to be honest and say that it does read pretty negatively, but I am only trying to make you aware of the pitfalls in advance. The idea of becoming a breeder of Birman cats does sound fluffy and wonderful, but the reality can be anything but, and the last thing the world needs is more people breeding cats that may end up in rescue shelters.

It is essential that as breeders we health test and screen our cats and eliminate genetic weaknesses for the future of the breed. There are simply too many amateur breeders causing harm to the kitten mills that mass breed many cats for profit without the true care and attention the cats need.

If, however, you are passionate and willing to learn as much as you can from experts of the breed and have the financial resources, then why not? After all, I did it and I would love you to follow in my footsteps; the incredible pleasure and emotions I experienced over many years cannot be described. Please just be honest with yourself, and above all put the interests of the Birman cat first.

Chapter 3 - Cat Shows and Breeding Explained

These two topics are being put in the same chapter because most people who breed Birman cats either exhibit them or are regular attendees at cat shows.

For owners of pet Birmans, I would first turn to the breeder you bought your cat from and ask if your cat would be considered show quality and if your breeder would be willing to mentor you.

Photo Credit: Butch & Leanne Trabuc of Kanza Katz Cattery

The CFA and TICA offer mentor programs if the kitten's breeder is unable to help. It is possible to show cats if they are neutered or spayed. This separate category from intact cats is called Premiership in CFA and Alter class in TICA.

Some cat shows also offer a separate class for non-pedigreed cats known as Household Pets. Sometimes mismarked purebred cats or cats that otherwise do not fit within the breed standard (i.e., a tail kink, amputee, etc.) are also shown in the Household Pet division.

It is far easier to start showing with a kitten than to expect an older cat to accept the demands of a cat show. A cat has to be bathed, dried, and travel to a large venue where other cats, strangers, and a public address system can be very stressful to the non-indoctrinated cat.

Birmans are a very cooperative breed and show well, but this fact doesn't alter the major differences in how cats are shown as opposed to dogs.

Dogs are rarely crated at shows and happily walk around on their leads or lie patiently at their owner's feet. You'll also see show dogs being groomed and fluffed up without complaint.

Cats are crated *all the time*. They'll stage a jailbreak in an instant, as evidenced by the dreaded cry of "loose cat!" Show cats may be forced to endure being combed and groomed before going into the ring, but they clearly are not having the time of their lives; if you have an exception to this rule you are lucky!

How Cat Shows Work

For all these differences and for the cats' minimal agreement with the nonsense, a cat show is a festive affair. Since the animals are only removed from their cages for judging, exhibitors go all out decorating their assigned area.

Attendees stroll up and down admiring both the cats and the displays. Everything seems calm and pleasant, but there's always a frantic undercurrent. Long periods of boredom are punctuated by mad dashes to the ring.

You will find vendors for all things feline taking advantage of the slow pace. It's extremely easy to spend a lot of money at cat shows, but it's not generally an adoption venue or even a place to negotiate a potential purchase for kittens, although sometimes there are shelter cats for adoption in the lobby or in an adjacent room to the cat show venue.

Entrants are judged according to formalized breed standards drawn up by the governing body for the show. Each organization may have slightly different rules, but the show standards are essentially uniform.

The major organizations in the cat fancy are:

- American Association of Cat Enthusiasts
- American Cat Fanciers' Association
- The International Cat Association
- Governing Council of the Cat Fancy (GCCF)
- Fédération Internationale Féline
- World Cat Federation
- Cat Fanciers' Association
- Feline Federation Europe
- Australia Cat Federation

Understanding the Cat Show Atmosphere

There's one huge rule at cat shows. Don't touch. Yes, it's frustrating, but it's in place entirely for the protection of the cats. If you were to touch a cat suffering from an illness, and then touch a second animal, your hands could be the vectors for transmitting the illness.

If you are invited to pet one of the cats, you are being paid a supreme compliment, one delivered with a bottle of hand sanitizer. Don't be offended. Just use it. Remember, you're protecting the cat, not your own ego.

Also, never try to help in instances when a cat escapes. Just freeze in place. If you see the animal, quietly indicate its presence, but don't try to catch the runaway. You'll only add to the confusion and scare the cat more.

Stay out of the way at all times. It's quite common for a competitor rushing to the show ring to yell, "Right of way." When you hear that, move! Exhibitors only have a brief amount of time to get to the judging area or face disqualification. Keep your eyes and ears open and learn from what's going on around you. You can gain a great deal of information on individual breeds by listening to the comments the judges make as they are evaluating each animal.

Photo Credit: Margaret Wignall of Bijoubirmon Birmans

Tips & Advice From Linda Russell

Linda Russell of Jemley Birmans is also a committee member of the Birman Cat Club and she has extensive knowledge of showing Birmans. Here she kindly shares her tips and advice:

Visiting a show is a good first step. If you are thinking of exhibiting yourself you are going to need some show equipment and this is the perfect place to get your starter kit from many of the stalls available. For a relatively small expense you can purchase a white blanket, white litter tray, and white food and water dishes. Your cat litter needs to be pure white too. There should be no distinguishing added features so that your cat doesn't stand out in any way from the others. We advise always cleaning down the pen with bacterial wipes beforehand.

Send off for a couple of show schedules to familiarize yourself with the entry procedure. Take one to a show and by all means ask advice from any of the exhibitors to go through anything you are not sure of.

Entering a show is usually done well in advance, so it gives you plenty of time to prepare and work out your route to the venue. Prepare everything you need to take with you days beforehand so there is no chance of forgetting anything on the morning. Making sure your cat looks their best and a credit to you is a must.

On your arrival you will be asked to go through what we call 'Vetting In.' This is where a vet will check over your cat and make sure it's fit and healthy; this is to protect both your cat and any others of any infectious diseases. You will be asked to show your vaccination certificate as well, so making sure your cat is up to date with his or her booster is very important indeed.

Quite often you will be expected to be there early in the morning so you can have your cat all prepared and relaxed in his/her pen ready for the judging. This is usually when 'it's breakfast time' and a chance to socialize, wind down until it's time to go and check your results and see how well you have done!

Most of all, enjoy the day. They always say 'You take the best cat home' and this, we find, is perfectly true!

The Birman Breed Group Show Standard (USA)

Judging in cat shows is a complicated business requiring judges to learn intricate breed standards. The actual awarding of ribbons and trophies is based on the simple fact that the cats that most closely conform to the ideal standard receive the highest marks.

Ranking the cats, however, takes an experienced and practiced eye. To give you an idea of what is expected of a show-winning Birman, we have reproduced the scoring system and colors allowed for the CFA (Cat Fanciers' Association).

HEAD, BODY, TYPE & COAT (65 points).
Head (including boning, nose, jaw, chin profile, ear & eye shape & set) 30 points.
Body/Type (including boning, stockiness elongation, legs, tail) 25 Points.
Coat (including length, texture, ruff) 10 points.

COLOR – INCLUDING EYE COLOR (35 points)
Color except gloves (including body color, point color, eye color) 15 points.
Gloves (including front & rear gloves, laces & symmetry) 20 points.

COLOR EXCEPT GLOVES: Body: even, with subtle shading when allowed on all colors/patterns of more mature cats. Strong contrast between body color and points. Points except gloves: mask, ears, legs, and tail dense and clearly defined, all of the same shade. Mask covers entire face, including whisker pads, and is connected to ears by tracings. No ticking or white hair in points. Golden Mist: desirable in all points colors is the "golden mist," a faint golden beige cast on the back and sides. This is somewhat deeper in the seal points, and may be absent in kittens.

GLOVES: Front paws: front paws have white gloves ending in an even line across the paw at, or between, the second or third joints. (The third joint is where the paw bends when the cat is standing.) The upper limit of white should be the metacarpal (dew) pad. (The metacarpal pad is the highest up little paw pad, located in the middle of the back of the front paw, above the third joint and just below the wrist bones.) Symmetry of the front gloves is desirable. Back paws: white glove covers all the toes, and may extend up somewhat higher than front gloves. Symmetry of the rear gloves is desirable. Laces: the gloves on the back paws must extend up the back of the hock, and are called laces in this area. Ideally, the laces end in a point or inverted "V" and extend 1/2 to 3/4 of the way up the hock. Lower or higher laces are acceptable, but should not go beyond the hock. Symmetry of the two laces is desirable. Paw pads: pink preferred, but dark spot(s) on paw pad(s) acceptable because of the two colors in pattern. Note: ideally, the front gloves match, the back gloves match, and the two laces match. Faultlessly gloved cats are a rare exception, and the Birman is to be judged in all its parts, as well as the gloves.

PENALIZE: White that does not run across the front paws in an even line. Lack of white on all front toes. Persian or Siamese type head. Delicate bone structure. White shading on stomach and chest. Lack of laces on one or both back gloves. White beyond the metacarpal (dew) pad. (The metacarpal pad is the highest up little paw pad, located in the middle of the back of the front paw, above the third joint and just below the wrist bones.)

DISQUALIFY: Lack of white gloves on any paw. Kinked or abnormal tail. Structural defects or abnormalities. Crossed eyes. Incorrect number of toes. Areas of pure white in the points, if not connected to the gloves and part of or an extension of the gloves. Paw pads are part of the gloves. Areas of white connected to other areas of white by paw pads (of any color) are not cause for disqualification. Discrete areas of point color in the gloves, if not connected to point color of legs (exception, paw pads). White on back legs beyond the hock. Eye color other than blue. White tail tips or chin spots.

BIRMAN COLORS

SEAL POINT: Body even pale fawn to cream, warm in tone, shading gradually to lighter color on the stomach and chest. Points, except for gloves, deep seal brown. Nose leather: same color as points.

BLUE POINT: Body bluish white to pale ivory, shading gradually to almost white on stomach and chest. Points, except for gloves, slate blue. Nose leather: slate blue.

CHOCOLATE POINT: Body ivory. Points, except for gloves, milk chocolate color, warm in tone. Nose leather: cinnamon pink.

LILAC POINT: Almost white. Points, except for gloves, frosty grey with pinkish tone. Nose leather: lavender-pink.

Tabby Point Color Classes

There should be a clearly defined "M" marking on the forehead, light colored "spectacle" markings around the eyes with spotted whisker pads. Ears solid with no stripes. "Thumb marks," which are less apparent in dilute colors and kittens, should be visible on the back of the ears. Ear furnishings in front of the ears should be off white in color. The legs should have clearly defined, varied sized broken stripes and/or rings. There should be solid markings on the back of the hind legs above the laces. A tail showing lighter and darker rings is preferred, but such markings may only occur on the underside and should not then be faulted. The tail may be ticked. The chin may be light colored but not white. A light-colored "bow tie" should be evident just below the nose.

Seal Tabby Point Color Class

SEAL TABBY POINT: Body even pale fawn to cream, warm in tone, shading gradually to lighter color on the stomach and chest. Pale body coat is desirable, preferably free from body markings; however, body shading of light ghost striping toning with the points is acceptable. Points, except for gloves, seal brown markings on a pale brown agouti background. Solid marking on back of hind legs should be deep seal brown. Tail color, with the exception of the rings, should be deep seal brown. Nose leather: pink to brick colored outlined in seal to tone with the points. A solid color nose leather to tone with the point color is acceptable.

Blue Tabby Point Color Class

BLUE TABBY POINT: Body bluish white to pale ivory, shading gradually to almost white on stomach and chest. Pale body coat is desirable, preferably free from body markings; however, body shading of light ghost striping toning with the points is acceptable. Points, except for gloves, blue markings on a light beige agouti background. Solid markings on back of hind legs should be solid blue. Tail color, with the exception of the rings, should be blue. Nose leather: pink to brick colored outlined in blue to tone with the points. A solid color nose leather to tone with the point color is acceptable.

Other Tabby Point Colors Class

CHOCOLATE TABBY POINT: Body ivory with little shading. Pale body coat is desirable, preferably free from body markings; however, body shading of light ghost striping toning with the points is acceptable. Points, except for gloves, milk chocolate markings on a light bronze agouti background. Solid markings on the back of the hind legs should be a milk chocolate color, warm in tone. Tail color, with the exception of the rings, should be milk chocolate in color. Nose leather: pink to brick colored outlined in chocolate to tone with the points. A solid color nose leather to tone with the point color is acceptable.

LILAC TABBY POINT: Body almost white (magnolia color). Pale body coat is desirable, preferably free from body markings; however, body shading of light ghost striping toning with the points is acceptable. Points, except for gloves, frosty grey with pinkish tone markings on a pale beige agouti background. Solid markings on the back of the hind legs should be frosty grey with a pinkish tone. Tail color, with the exception of the rings, should be frosty grey with a pinkish tone. Nose leather: pink to brick colored outlined in grey-pink to tone with the points. A solid color nose leather to tone with the point color is acceptable.

RED TABBY POINT: Body creamy white, shading gradually to white on stomach and chest. Pale body coat is desirable, preferably free from body markings; however, body shading of light ghost striping toning with the points is acceptable. Points, except for gloves, deep red on a light apricot agouti background. Solid markings on the back of the hind legs should be deep red. The tail color, with the exception of the rings, should be deep red. Nose leather: pink to brick colored outlined in red to tone with the points. A solid color nose leather to tone with the point color is acceptable.

CREAM TABBY POINT: Body clear white to creamy with no shading. Pale body coat is desirable, preferably free from body markings; however, body shading of light ghost striping toning with the points is acceptable. Thumb marks are less apparent in cream tabby points. Points, except for gloves, buff cream on a paler cream agouti background. Solid markings on the back of the hind legs should be buff cream. Nose leather: pink to brick colored outline in cream to tone with the points. A solid color nose leather to tone with the point color is acceptable. NOTE: on red and cream tabby points, "freckles" may occur on nose, lips, eyelids and ears. Slight freckling in a mature cat should not be penalized.

SEAL-TORTIE TABBY POINT: Body mottled pale fawn to creamy white, shading gradually to lighter color on stomach and chest. Thumb marks are mottled in seal-tortie tabby points. Points, except for gloves, seal brown markings on a pale brown agouti background overlaid and intermingled with shades of light and dark red. Nose leather: pink, mottled pink or seal.

CHOCOLATE-TORTIE TABBY POINT: Body mottled ivory to creamy white, shading gradually to white on stomach and chest. Thumb marks are mottled in chocolate-tortie tabby points. Points, except for gloves, milk chocolate markings on a light bronze agouti background overlaid and intermingled with shades of light and dark red. Nose leather: pink, mottled pink and chocolate or solid chocolate.

BLUE-CREAM TABBY POINT: Body mottled bluish white to clear white, shading gradually to almost white on stomach and chest. Points, except for gloves, blue markings on a light beige agouti background overlaid and intermingled with shades of light and dark cream. Nose leather: pink, mottled pink and blue or solid blue.

LILAC-CREAM TABBY POINT: Body almost white with no shading. Points, except for gloves, lilac markings on a pale beige agouti background overlaid and intermingled with shades of cream. Nose leather: pink, mottled pink and light grey or solid pink-grey. NOTE: the four colors above show the normal tabby point pattern which has been overlaid with shades of light and dark red (seal-tortie/chocolate-tortie) or cream (blue-cream/lilac-cream). The extent and distribution of the tortie areas are not important providing that both elements, tortie and tabby, are clearly visible.

Photo Credit: Jan & Merle Shelton of Templkatz Birmans

Parti-Color Colors Class

SEAL-TORTIE POINT: Body mottled pale fawn to creamy white, shading gradually to lighter color on stomach and chest. Points, except for gloves, seal brown, mottled with red. Nose leather: in accordance with one or both point colors.

BLUE-CREAM POINT: Body mottled slate bluish white to clear white, shading gradually to almost white on stomach and chest.

Points, except for gloves, slate blue mottled with cream. Nose leather: in accordance with one or both point colors.

CHOCOLATE-TORTIE POINT: Body mottled ivory to creamy white, shading gradually to white on stomach and chest. Points, except for gloves, milk chocolate mottled with red. Nose leather: in accordance with one or both point colors.

LILAC-CREAM POINT: Body almost white with no shading. Points, except for gloves, frosty gray with pinkish tone, mottled with cream. Nose leather: in accordance with one or both point colors.

Other Solid Point Colors Class

RED POINT: Body creamy white, shading gradually to white on stomach and chest. Points, except for gloves, deep red. Nose leather: bright pink.

CREAM POINT: Body creamy white to clear white with no shading. Points, except for gloves, buff cream. Nose leather: flesh pink. NOTE: on red points and cream points, small dark "freckles" may occur on nose, lips, eyelids and ears. Slight freckling in a mature cat should not be penalized.

The Birman Breed Group Show Standard (UK)

The Supreme Cat show is the feline equivalent of the world famous "Crufts Dog Show" in the United Kingdom. It is not an impossible dream to show your Birman—anybody can start up this wonderful hobby; the GCCF in the UK runs the "YES" scheme to encourage the younger exhibitors. It is possible to show with a pedigreed or a non-pedigreed cat; it is your choice.

Before making your decision, attend a show or two before

making your choice, and if you do decide to go ahead, with a pedigreed cat, choose a breeder who is prepared to mentor you and help and guide you at the start.

To be successful at a cat show the exhibit needs to be in prime health and condition, and needs to be well-handled and preferably have a social and outgoing personality. Cats that do particularly well are those who enjoy being show-offs and love the attention they receive at the shows. For pedigreed cats they must adhere to the standard of points again provided by the Governing Council of the Cat Fancy (GCCF):

The exhibitor needs to be prepared to be gracious in defeat and always remember to congratulate others. Showing Birmans must be a daily labor of love, grooming, nutrition and general well-being, play being an important part of the day for their development—all are of paramount importance. Fail to prepare, prepare to fail.

Here is the UK breed standard as reproduced in full from: http://birmancatclub.co.uk/pdf/sop.pdf

GENERAL TYPE STANDARD:

Head: Skull strong, broad and rounded. Nose medium in length (no 'stop' but with slight dip in profile). Cheeks full and round tapering to a strong, well-developed muzzle. Chin full and well developed.

Ears: Medium in size and spaced well apart.

Eyes: Almost round but not bold. Blue in color, the deeper the blue the better.

Body: Long and large, well boned and of good substance for age.

Legs and Paws: Legs of medium length and thick set, paws short and strong.

Tail: Bushy, and in proportion to the body.

Coat & Condition: Coat long, silken in texture, full ruff around the neck, slightly curled on stomach. Eyes bright and temperament good.

Color: The distinguishing colors of the Birman are those of the Siamese. Mask, ears, legs and tail dense and clearly defined (except in kittens). On reaching maturity, the mask covers the entire face, including whisker pads, and is connected to the ears by tracings.

The white feet are characteristic of the Birman:

Front Paws: Have pure white symmetrical gloves ending in an even line across the paw and not passing beyond the angle formed by the paw and leg, and not passing the stopper pad just behind the leg. Color of the paw pads irrelevant.

Back Paws: Have pure white socks covering the entire paw and gauntlets tapering up the back of the leg to finish just below the point of the hock. Color of the paw pads irrelevant.

SCALE OF POINTS:
Head and ears 20
Eyes 15
Body, Legs & paws 20
Gloves & Gauntlets 5
Tail 20
Color and Condition of Coat 20
Total: 100

Chapter 4 - Daily Care for Your Birman

As you embark on this new adventure with a Birman kitten, give your kitten plenty of time to adjust to his new surroundings and he will be prepared to give you years of love, attention, entertainment, and companionship.

The first thing people ask about any breed of cat they want to adopt is something like, "Do they have a good personality?" What they don't seem to realize is that cats are individuals, too. It's absolutely ridiculous to assume that all cats of the same breed will behave identically under all circumstances.

Photo Credit: Marilyn Rowley of Barmar Birmans

Animals, like people, are influenced by the manner in which they are raised and the environment in which they live. While it is true that the vast majority of Birmans are easygoing, laid back, sociable cats, I knew one woman who was bitterly disappointed when she adopted one that was shy and retiring.

The Birman in question was also the runt of the litter, was adopted from a questionable cattery at too young an age, and taken into a household filled with loud noises without proper socialization – and forced to live with an elderly, very alpha Siamese who was determined to be an only child!

I have to confess I wasn't all that sympathetic about the woman's complaints, although I did facilitate placing the cat in another home. It was absurd for this person, who in my opinion had no business owning cats at all, to assume that everything was the poor Birman's fault. The animal was completely overwhelmed by its environment and didn't get much if any help from its less than understanding human!

Although I completely reject the notion of "one personality fits all" for any breed, I can make a few selective observations about life with a Birman. I do not, however, think it's a good idea to begin a relationship with any animal based on preset expectations. All friendships, including those with companion animals, are strongest when they are allowed to evolve naturally.

Are Birmans Selective with Their Affection?

Of course cats are selective with their affections! Aren't you? It is true that some breeds, including the Birman, have a reputation for high sociability. I have found, however, in more than 50 years of living with cats, that all of them have a tendency to single out one person as "theirs." Birmans do it too.

This doesn't mean they aren't fantastic family cats, it just means they're "human" and they do have favorites. If you're that person, you're very lucky! If you're not, you'll still have perfectly delightful interactions with these cordial and good-natured felines.

When you have earned the love and trust of a Birman, they are devoted companions who like to be near their people without getting all clingy. Like most cats, Birmans enjoy their lap time, but they're good with camping out on the end of the couch while you read.

They like attention, but they don't get bent out of shape when you're not constantly cooing over them. Basically, this breed leans toward being really well adjusted!

Can a Birman ignore you when you've annoyed him? Absolutely! He's a cat down to the tufts of his toes! But it's extremely rare for a Birman to get bent out of shape enough to really display any temper.

Yes, he might stalk off and be aloof for a bit, but in the end, his native good nature and curiosity will get the best of him and he'll come back in and do something goofy, restoring his good humor and yours in one fell swoop.

Aren't All Cats Loners?

Some cats are loners in that they prefer their one special person and hold themselves apart when visitors are around. The Birman isn't typically one of those cats, however.

Your pet will be glad to see you at the end of the day, but once he knows your schedule, he'll be fine on his own for a few hours while you're at work.

Cats Have Emotional and Physical Needs

Having a cat for a pet involves more than putting out food and water and changing the litter box. A lot of people who adopt a cat for the first time do so with some serious misconceptions about their new pet's real and decided emotional needs.

If you are not prepared to spend time with your Birman to make him part of the family (even if you're single), to pay for appropriate veterinary care, and to devote the required time to grooming, then reconsider your choice of companion animal.

Bringing Your New Cat Home

One of the things I especially enjoy about Birmans is their propensity for being adaptable. They do quite well with other pets, even dogs, and are good with children, removing themselves without fuss if something's going on they don't like.

But even given all that, Birmans are cats, and like all members of their species, they do like the major parts of their world to stay the same. No cat is ever happy with change.

You can't just throw a cat into a household without some issues. The majority—especially if there are other animals in the house—need time to adjust in a smaller environment. It's important to let them adjust on their own time. If they need to hide to feel safe for several days, then let them do it. Pulling them out from under a bed to cuddle them scares them more. Cats are animals that need to come to you on their own.

It's important to do a good job managing your kitten's transition from life at the cattery to your household. The move can be intimidating if not handled correctly, and disaster can ensue in two vital aspects of feline life: the litter box and the food bowl.

All new kittens should start out in a room and not be allowed to have full access to the house until he/she is comfortable. If a home has multiple levels, there should be a litter box on each floor, as kittens have short-term memories and get distracted easily, like a small child. The litter box can be moved to the basement if desired after the kitten is about 6 months old.

Photo Credit: Ann Mott of Jandouglen Birmans

Let the Breeder Guide You

By this point in my comments on transitioning a kitten, it should be clear to you that I believe you should be guided in the beginning by the breeder's recommendations, even if you fancy yourself to be an old hand with cats.

You have to remember that the breeder doesn't just know Birmans, he or she also knows the individual kitten you will be caring for. The breeder will likely suggest some things like:

- Keeping the baby segregated in a small, quiet area for a few days, especially if there are other pets in the house. Companion animals tend to do best together when they are given a chance to introduce themselves with a paw under the door and a lot of exploratory smelling.

- Ensure kitty feels secure and warm by providing a cardboard box lined with a blanket or a store-bought bed to cozy up in. As they can sleep for as much as sixteen hours a day, this is important!

Please do not let your kitten sleep with you in the bedroom unless you are absolutely sure that you will allow this forever. Once your kitten sleeps with you, he will never want to sleep anywhere else.

- Keep necessary items close by, including the litter tray, clean water and a bowl of food.

- Supervising face-to-face meetings with existing pets, but not overreacting. Animals pick up on our emotions. Your pets will work out a pecking order, and even though Birmans are calm by nature, they are still cats with claws—needle-sharp claws when you're talking about kittens.

Introduce your kitten to the safe room first. Take the carrier into the room, open the carrier, and leave. Give him plenty of time to explore it—he is looking for hidden dangers and hiding places.

Your kitten will be lonely and cry for you once he has explored his new space. Go into the room, talk to him in a high-pitched voice, sit, and wait for him to come to you. When your kitten is frightened, his natural instinct is to hide. Let the kitten hide! The worst thing you can do is to pull the kitten out of the hiding place and try to comfort him. You are precisely what he is afraid of, and forcing him to confront you will not help.

Kittens vary in their adjustment to a new home. He may come running right over to you. But if he's shy, he may just poke his head out and view you from a distance. Spend 5 minutes in the room, and then leave again for 10 minutes. Each time you go back, your kitten will be braver.

The way to a kitten's heart is through play! Once your kitten calms down, try to coax him out with a toy, and play with him. Once your kitten consistently comes toward you as soon as you enter, purring, tail up over his back, he has started to bond with you. At this point you can quietly, slowly introduce other humans to him in the safe room.

You will bond with your new kitten much more quickly through play than through cuddling. After playing, when your kitten is relaxed and tired, cuddling will be most welcome.

Resist the temptation to invite the neighborhood over to see your new pet. Give him time to become comfortable in his new home.

- Older cats may be threatened by a new kitten. Allow the older cat to smell the kitten, and should they fight, separate them immediately.

- Keep dogs on a lead initially. Don't worry, cats and dogs do co-exist just fine.

Of course you want to intervene if necessary, but pecking orders have a way of forming on their own and sometimes it's the new kid on the block that's in charge!

- Although initially everyone is excited and will want to hold the new kitten, it is best to introduce one person at a time and limit picking up, as it can be intimidating at first, until your new pet settles in.

- Let your kitten decide when the time is right to explore the rest of the house by leaving the door open, and make sure you pop in to say hello as often as you can in the early days.

- Don't bring your new kitten home and then go out to work the next day. Make sure you are able to be at home for the first couple of days at the very least. A weekend is best.

- Establish a sleeping routine by closing the door to her room. Otherwise she will be jumping on your bed or playing in the middle of the night. Don't give in if you hear crying or scratching and soon she will give up, and it will become a set routine.

After a week to 10 days the kitten should be completely adjusted to the transition and ready to venture into larger areas of your home, which means you will need to do some kitten proofing.

Birmans and Other Pets

Introduce your Birman to other pets in the house via paws under the door and a lot of exploratory sniffing. When face-to-face meetings are attempted for the first time, it's important for you not to overreact to any paw slapping that take place. Animals pick up on our emotions and without meaning to, you could negatively influence the whole interaction.

Animals in multi-pet households work out their own pecking order. Even as young cats, Birmans are calm and genial by nature, but they still have claws. In kittens, those claws are sharp as needles. Don't be surprised if it's your older cats that backs away yelping after getting nailed by a slap from a little hissing ball of fur!

Clearly if these first meetings get out of hand you'll need to intervene, but after about a week to 10 days everything should be settled down. Once your kitten is ready to venture into the larger parts of the house, however, you will need to make sure you've kitten proofed those areas.

The Transitional Litter Box

The kitten you adopt should be accustomed to using a litter pan, but cats are incredibly particular about their "bathrooms." You need to make sure you don't do anything to confuse a young cat and set back its training in this regard.

Find out the type of box and litter the breeder has been using with the cat and replicate the arrangement exactly. When the kitten first moves into your home, keep it confined to a limited area and provide it with one litter box.

Photo Credit: Linda Russell of Jemley Birmans

As you gradually allow the cat to have the run of the house, consider providing a second box. The general rule of thumb is to have one more pan than there are cats in the house.

If at any point you decide to use a different type of litter box or litter, make the change very slowly and don't discard the original items until your cat is comfortable with the new arrangement and doing his "business" there routinely.

The Transitional Menu

In the matter of your kitten's food bowl, again, find out what the breeder has been using and present your new cat with exactly the same type of bowl and the same food. The last thing you want is to trigger some kind of gastrointestinal upset.

The breeder will likely have good suggestions about how the kitten's diet should change as it grows. You can also discuss food choices with your vet, and I will be talking more about nutrition shortly. Just remember that all cats are carnivores. The quality of any food that doesn't list meat as the main ingredient should be considered suspect.

Have plenty of toys waiting for your new baby. Pay attention to what the cat does and doesn't like. These observations will guide your future purchases. Just make sure that none of the items present a choking hazard. Don't bother with catnip. Kittens don't react to "kitty weed" before the age of 6–9 months.

Starting a Grooming Routine

You should start a combing and brushing routine with your Birman kitten immediately. The breeder will already have been doing this with the cat and it's imperative that you not fall down on the schedule.

Find out the type of implements the breeder has been using and when and under what conditions the grooming has been done. If the kitten is used to sitting on someone's lap in the evenings for brushing, do the same thing.

With every element of the kitten's daily routine—litter box, diet, and grooming—you are trying to emphasize continuity and give the baby a sense of "life as usual."

Kitten Proofing

If you just read that header and thought, "Why would I need to kitten proof?" you may not have ever lived with a kitten! They are a force of nature with which to be reckoned. Think two tons of curiosity that looks like a powder puff.

What I find so beguiling about kittens is that they have no concept of being small. Perhaps you've seen the poster of the tiny yellow kitten looking into a mirror and seeing a lion looking back? Nothing could be more accurate!

Get down on the floor at kitten level and have a look around. Try to put yourself in the mind of a pint-sized Birman on a mission to discover what's new in the world.

See that cord to the TV? Tape it to the baseboard. Do the same with every other electrical cord in the room. And for good measure, cap the outlets.

Not only are cords dangerous for your baby cat to chew on, they can also be used to pull down or tip over heavy and dangerous objects. At least in the beginning, I recommend removing all house plants from any area to which the kitten has access. There are more plants that are toxic to cats than those that are not. I have personally instituted a "no plants allowed" policy in my home. If you do want to keep plants, research each one for potential toxicity.

Also, apply baby latches to any cabinet doors, especially those where any type of chemicals are being stored. Birmans get less nosy and curious as they age, but kittens will definitely be kittens.

Keep small items that could be swallowed locked away, and definitely no plastic bags lying around. Keep the toilet lid down and the dishwasher and washing machine door closed at all times!

Climbing

Birman kittens often go through a period of climbing everything in sight, including curtains, drapes and legs. You will not be able to teach your kitten not to do this because they do this to protect themselves in the wild. However, the good news is that he will usually stop by 6–8 months, when he grows in size and confidence.

Communicating in "Birman"

The extent to which a Birman uses its voice is completely individualistic, but overall, this is a chatty breed given to melodic chirping and trilling. They are conversational, but pleasantly so and not at all raucous.

I'd like to be able to give you a dictionary for "cat," but their language is not limited to vocalizations. It's a complex mixture of signals comprising expressions, body language, scents, and sounds. Language experts guess that cats can pick up a working vocabulary of about 25–30 words from us, but they can emit about 100 sounds of their own. Just as a basis for comparison, it's estimated that dogs learn around 100 words, yet they make only 15 sounds. That theorizing is all well and good, but I wonder if those experts have ever actually lived with a cat or a dog.

I work from home and spend an enormous amount of time talking to my cats. I assure you they know far more than 25–30 words. The real issue in communicating with a cat isn't his comprehension but rather a matter of how you get his attention.

These animals don't ignore us because they are by nature arrogant. While it's true that you've never really *been* ignored until you've been ignored by a cat, the real reason Fluffy doesn't hang on your every word is that he may not be able to hear what you're saying.

Cats do have very acute hearing, but it's designed to pick up high-pitched sounds like a mouse squeaking behind the wall on the other side of the living room. Cats often don't pay attention to us when we talk to them because much of human speech drops below the frequencies their ears are built to pick up on.

To them, we must sound like little more than a dull roar. Yelling at a cat gets you nowhere, but see what happens when you whisper. His ears will go up, his eyes will dilate, and he'll look right at you. Pair soft-voiced commands with hand signals that capitalize on a cat's instinct to learn body language and you'll be shocked at how effecting your "commands" will be.

You can try your sternest voice when you tell a Birman or any other cat to get "down," but in all likelihood you'll be confronted with an impassive and vaguely bored stare. But say the word "down" softly and punctuate it by sternly pointing at the floor and Fluffy will generally do as you ask.

Do not, however, assume that your cats can't or won't pick up on and learn your spoken language. Again, you must remember that all cats are *individuals*. I had a gray and white American Shorthair tom with a vocabulary so extensive, I often caught him responding to things I said to someone else over the telephone.

Photo Credit: Paula & James Watson of Bitaheaven Birmans

I do believe that my cats and I "converse" unusually well. I spend a lot of time with them and I do talk to them. (Yes, I do realize this sounds a little daft.) But I think the more you expose an intelligent animal to any type of communication—whether that be words or hand signals—the more you both will learn about how the other communicates. After all, the word "communication" does imply a two-way exchange of information, so you have some things to learn as well.

To that end, let's consider some of the fundamentals of speaking "cat."

- A cat with wide-open eyes and small pupils is calm and interested.

- The same wide-eyed cat with large pupils is afraid.
- When a cat's eyes go "hard" he's not only interested, but also focused and likely ready to pounce on something he sees as "prey."
- Narrowed eyes paired with a lashing tail and ears that are back and flat clearly signal a warning, "Back off."
- A cat striding along with his tail flipped up and forward is relaxed and in a good mood.

There are two sounds that all cats make that I really love. The first you'll hear most often when your pet is sitting with face pressed to the window staring at a bird or a squirrel. It's sort of a chattering teeth clacking often accompanied with a short little bark. It's basically cat for, "Wow! Mom! Look!"

And that signature "meow" that you think is your cat speaking to you? Uh. Okay. Brace yourself. Adult cats don't meow at one another, so when your cat does send a meow in your direction, it's treating you like a kitten in need of placation or correction. Yes, our cats really do see us that way!

I love a Birman's capacity for wordless "conversations." Like other Oriental breeds, they have terrific intuition and powers of observation, correctly zeroing in on subtle nuances of mood. Many dog people are quite taken aback to hear that cats know and care when their people have had a bad day, but it's true. Don't be at all surprised to find your Birman snuggled up beside you offering comfort when you come home emotionally bruised from a lousy day on the job.

Interaction and Play

Birmans love to play but don't think it's necessary to spend a lot of money on purchasing toys—your Birman kitten is likely to play with everyday items just lying around the house.

Toys to avoid include bells that might detach and be swallowed and feathers, as the quill can become stuck in a cat's throat if they chew them. Watch out for toys that dangle from elastic strings. Keep small objects such as safety pins, pins, paper clips, buttons, bobby pins, rubber bands, thread, etc. away from your kitten.

Uncooked pasta makes a great toy, as well as ping pong balls, shoe laces, a rolled up sock, practice golf balls (lightweight, plastic, with holes in them) and rolled up tin foil or paper.

A laser pen is a wonderful toy for the kitten and good exercise. They will happily chase it for quite some time, but avoid the face because lasers can damage eyes.

Primarily, a Birman is just happy to be spending time with you. I always counsel new cat parents regardless of the breed they've adopted to just watch your pet and get to know what interests and intrigues him. It's not a huge problem for a few introductory toys to go ignored until you find just the right thing. I have one male who thinks a crumpled up grocery store receipt on a hardwood floor is the best cat toy ever!

Birmans are not aloof loners. They're goofy pals. They'll show you what they like and don't like. They're just as capable of being stubborn as any other cat, but they tend to be fairly nice about it. This is, however, an extremely intelligent breed and they respond well to learning routines and "tricks."

That should not, however, be a forced thing. I don't advocate presenting any cat with a class schedule of "tricks," and then trying to get him to study and pass the test. That just doesn't go well in my experience. I prefer to get to know my cats and then create both games and tricks that match the individual's interests and tastes.

One of my smartest cats turned doorknobs with his paws and loved for me to close the bedroom door so he could prove it to me—over and over again.

Another liked a version of the old "shell game." He had an exceptional memory and was adept at opening boxes. I'd show him a toy, then turn around and hide the item in one of several boxes. Invariably he'd walk straight to the right box and retrieve the toy. It was almost spooky. Like most cats, his attention span lasted about 15 minutes and then it was time for a nap, but he never tired of playing the game one more time.

Rewarding positive behavior is the foundation of all animal training. Birmans are incredibly loyal companions and are very affectionate, with their reward typically just being with you. Just spend time interacting with and getting to know your cats. The games and tricks will evolve naturally.

Birmans love the kitty shelves and hammocks you can install on a window sill and they love their cat tree, but these are not necessary, as without them they will find their own favorite spot.

Photo Credit: Linda Russell of Jemley Birmans

Tickling

Although it is fun when your kitten is very young, do not tickle his stomach to the point that he scratches and bites. If he does this then know that he is just following natural instinct and simulating killing a small animal. If he continues to treat hands this way when he gets bigger, he may hurt you or an unsuspecting child. Replace your delicate hand with a stuffed toy or a pair of socks, and let him scratch and fight that.

Scruffing

When the mother cat carries her babies around by the scruff of the neck, they relax, knowing they are safe and protected. Because of this your kitten will automatically relax if you scratch the back of his neck or scruff him. If he is ever injured, frightened, or aggressive, scruff him to alleviate the situation. This controls and calms your cat with one hand without any danger from being bitten or scratched.

Scratching

None of my Birman cats or kittens has ever developed the habit of clawing or scratching furniture or carpeting, but cats will want to scratch. It's a fact of life with a feline. Birmans don't have a reputation for being especially destructive with their claws, they just need pointing in the right direction and a scratching post is an essential purchase.

Your Birman is not being bad when they scratch. Their need to clean and sharpen their claws is instinctual. With the right training, this is no more an issue than litter box management, but part of the responsibility does fall to you.

Keep your kitten's nails clipped. Use nail clippers from a pet store that are designed specifically for cats. Don't clip the nails too close, or they will bleed and hurt, and your cat will be wise to it next time and object before you even start. Just remove the very tip, the sharp part of the nail.

A simple scratching pole that costs $30/£20 will generally suffice for a Birman, but you need to buy the tallest, sturdiest one in the store. It must be at least as tall as the cat is when the cat is stretched to full height, up on his hind legs. Rub catnip into the post when you first get it. Add new catnip every few weeks if necessary.

I must admit that all of mine have access to rather elaborate cat trees with perches, tunnels, ramps, and observation platforms. These units set me back $100 – $300 (£65 – £197) each, but I'm happy with this expenditure because in my opinion they're worth it for the high interest level, the fun my cats have and the added exercise they get.

When problem scratching of furniture is an issue, I recommend applying either pennyroyal or orange essence spray as a deterrent. Remember, cats have fantastically acute noses and they hate both of these scents. I've used both and have not had any trouble with fabric staining, but always perform a test application on a small, unobtrusive area first. Each of these mixtures sell for $12–$15 / £7.87–£9.84.

Catnip encourages scratching, so be sure to keep catnip away from upholstered furniture and carpet. DO rub catnip on the scratching post from time to time.

The corrugated cardboard scratchers are inexpensive and excellent, impregnated with catnip. Posts wrapped in sisal rope are an even better and sturdier choice.

One of my adopted Birmans clearly had a carpet scratching habit—I acquired a small carpet sample in a contrasting color, and she immediately switched to scratching on it and never bothered the carpet or sofa again.

As a last resort, you can have little shields glued to the ends of your Birman's front claws. These will prevent all damage to carpeting and upholstery.

Double-sided adhesive strips are also an excellent and affordable deterrent for scratching because cats dislike the "tacky" feeling on their paws. The strips sell for around $8–$10 / £5.25–£6.56.

The best way to prevent your cat from scratching the furniture is to provide something else that is more fun to scratch.

Joann Lamb has this to say: "I keep a scratching post in every room of the house. Some are attached to cat trees, others are small, free-standing sisal posts. I have never had a Birman scratch my furniture."

Corrective Training

As a last resort, if you really must teach your kitten not to do something, the best method I have found is a plant sprayer/mister with water in it. Try not to let the kitten associate the unpleasant spraying with you. Being sprayed, very lightly, is so unpleasant to a cat that the mere sight of the bottle will soon stop bad behaviors. This method can also be useful if you have other cats coming into your house via the cat flap.

Chapter 5 - Litter Box Training For Your Birman

One reason cats are so popular as companions is the fact that they can live inside and take care of their elimination needs in a pan of sand or gravel. Not only does kitty not have to be taken for walks outside, he'd have no part of such nonsense anyway. Actually that's something of a myth because many cats, Birmans included, will agreeably walk on a leash if the training is begun at an early age. Fit your cat with a harness rather than a collar if you want to teach it to walk on a lead.

Photo Credit: Dawn Brown of Dalteema Birmans

Ideally your Birman should come to you litter box trained so that your primary responsibility is one of maintenance and reinforcing good habits. If, however, you do have to introduce a kitten to a litter box, the process goes something like this.

- Fill a pan with sand or gravel litter.
- Put the kitten in the pan.

- Gently take its front paws and make a digging motion for a few strokes.

The cat will take it from there. By nature cats are absolutely fastidious creatures. They come pre-programmed to dig, do their business, and cover. Show them where they have soft "dirt" to do that and the rest is pure instinct on their part.

Many cats are given up for problems related to litter box use, a fact that causes me equal parts aggravation and sadness—know that there is always a reason (medical, environmental or psychological) for a change in litter habits.

Cats are so clean by nature that if they go "off" their litter pan the cause is likely a physical problem like a urinary infection or a bladder blockage. The first step in addressing the issue is to take the cat to the vet!

Reason through the issue like a cat. You go into the pan to do what you need to do. It hurts. In cat logic, you try to find a place next time that doesn't hurt! The cat associates the location with the pain and tries to avoid the pain.

If there is no physical ailment, then consider your own responsibility for what's happened. If you aren't doing a good job of maintaining the box, the cat may be refusing to use the site because it's just too disgusting.

Humans have roughly 5 million receptors for odor sensing. Cats have 200 million. If you think something smells offensive, to a cat it's absolutely repugnant. Is it any wonder he doesn't want to go in a filthy litter box?

Consider if you've changed anything recently.

Does the kitten feel safe where the litter is? Is it easily accessible? Is one of your other pets terrorizing your kitten when you are not watching?

Was there a major change in your kitten's life? New food? New pet? Work schedule suddenly means you're rarely at home? Strong chemicals (e.g. insecticides) used near the litter box?

Did the kitty litter get moved? Cats remember the location, not the color and size of the litter box. Your new kitten can handle only so much change at a time.

Does the box have a cover on it? Those can concentrate urine smell to the point that they sting your kitten's eyes. Try removing the cover and see whether the behavior changes.

Did you change to a different kind of litter? New litters should be slowly mixed with the old, gradually phasing out the type you are discontinuing. New boxes should be placed beside the old one until the animal is comfortable with the new arrangement. Abrupt changes typically result in abrupt reactions.

When changing litters to a completely different type (clay to clumping, or heavy clumping to something much lighter), another method is two litter boxes side by side. Become a little lax in keeping the old litter box quite as clean as the new, and the cat will naturally migrate to the new, cleaner litter box.

Kitty Litter

Be sure to keep the kitty litter clean. If you are planning to let your kitten sit on your lap and be cuddled, you probably want his litter to be clean. Modern litters may look dry on top, because wet waste is wicked to the bottom, but when the kitten scratches to cover or dig a hole, there may be nastiness underneath. This will discourage your kitten from using the litter box. Please check the cleanliness of the litter box often.

Preventing "Accidents"

If your Birman does go outside the litter pan, don't discipline the cat. Just get to work. You have some serious cleaning to do to prevent a recurrence. Remember, cats live in a world where scent is a major sensory experience.

When a cat urinates or defecates in a particular spot, in the future his nose will tell him that is now an acceptable place to "go." It is imperative that all traces of odor be removed with specialized enzymatic cleaners after such accidents.

I especially like a line of products for this purpose made by Nature's Miracle. They work exceedingly well and are affordably priced at $5–$10/£3–£6 per bottle.

Available Types of Litter

The traditional clay-based gravel is far from the only option now available to cat owners, but it is still very cheap, selling for just $2.50–$5.00 (£2–£4) per 10 lbs. (4.53 kg). Frankly, however, clay isn't ideal. It generates a terrific amount of dust and doesn't do a good job of absorbing urine, instead allowing wet puddles to accumulate in the bottom of the pan, which over time seep into the plastic. This creates an excessive ammonia odor that ultimately cannot be removed, and the wet litter is a real mess to clean up.

The preferred option for most cat people today is a clumping sand litter, which is both soft in texture and far less likely to cause "tracking" problems.

Old-style clay litters had a tendency to cling to the cat's feet and come off once the animal exits the box. This occurs less with sand, but vigorous scratchers can send plumes of the stuff flying, so be forewarned.

Clumping litters come in several different types, including multiple cat, odor control, and low dust—or some combination thereof. If you use sand, get a covered litter box to help keep the material more contained and consider putting the box on a rug or mat that you can carry outside and shake out from time to time.

Do not put clumps from the litter box in the toilet for flushing unless the box specifically says the material is "flushable." Otherwise, the litter will essentially harden to concrete in the pipes and utterly destroy your plumbing.

Although clumping litters are more expensive, they also return higher value in terms of efficiency, absorbency, and odor control. The litters are readily available in markets and grocery stores, selling for $18 / £12 for 42 lbs. (19 kg).

I know some people who have attempted to switch their cats over to plant-based eco-friendly litters that are biodegradable. I wholeheartedly applaud the concept, but my cats won't use the stuff at all.

These litters, which may be made of ground corn cobs or some type of wood shavings, are very lightweight. I don't think they feel substantial enough to the cat, plus the litter clings to the cat's fur. My cats were clearly annoyed by this fact and they proceeded to scatter the stuff all over the house.

Shaved pine is one example of an eco-friendly litter, selling for $10 / £7 per 20 lbs. (9.07 kg). I suppose if a cat were introduced to the material at a young age it might work, but I've had no success getting my cats to "go green."

Another biodegradable product, amorphous silica gel, is relatively new. The absorbent crystals in these products are intended to prevent urine puddles by trapping and absorbing the liquid and also inhibiting bacterial growth.

This is not a product I've tried personally, but several of my friends report that the texture is similar to that of gravel. Their cats were receptive to the crystals, which do exhibit superior absorbency over clumping litters. On average, you will pay $16 / £11 for 8 lbs.

Photo Credit: Sylvia Foulds of Angel Eyes Birmans

Selecting a Litter Box

There are three standard litter box configurations. In order of expense they are: open pan, covered box, and electric self-scooping.

Open plastic pans cost only $6–$10 / £4–£6 and have been used for years. It doesn't have to be a "litter box" from a pet store, you could use a dishpan or even a higher-sided plastic box/bin.

The two major disadvantages to this approach are unsightliness and the mess created by digging and covering. Some cats won't use anything else, however, so you are faced with using litter-trapping mats and placing the box in an out-of-the-way location or behind a screen.

Covered pans are far tidier and easier to place. For cats that prefer a sense of privacy, the arrangement is ideal. The vented lids include filters that help to control dust, but tracking and the occasional plume of litter out the entrance can still be problematic.

Another disadvantage is that because owners don't see them, they are not likely to be cleaned as often. Covered litter boxes also trap in aromas which some cats don't like. Many cats just prefer their boxes to be open.

These boxes can be purchased in almost any configuration from standard rectangles to triangles that fit neatly in corners. Size and shape determine price, but most fall in a range of $30–$50 / £20–£33.

Basically every cat owner sees a self-scooping box for the first time and wants it immediately. I bought one as soon as they came out. The idea is fantastic, and the boxes do work, but to be honest, the reception among my cats was mixed.

The function of the box works around a motion sensor triggered by the cat exiting the box. The signal activates a rake or a similar mechanism that combs through the used clumping litter to capture and remove the waste material, which is dumped into a closed receptacle.

When the bin is full, you empty it or throw the whole thing away. The unit I purchased used disposable plastic boxes with lids. (Not great environmentally, but a very contained solution.)

The box absolutely traumatized my youngest male. He would have no part of the "monster" and insisted on using a "normal" box. My "middle" boy was utterly fascinated. He came galloping to watch every time the elderly female used the box, which created a diplomatic situation because she demanded complete privacy.

We did continue to use the box, and subsequent cats that have been introduced to it as kittens are perfectly fine with it. Given that, if you want to go this route, introduce your cats to the automatic box as early in life as possible. Expect to pay $150–$200 (£98–£130) for one of these units.

Tidy Cats Breeze Litter Box System

If you have the budget for it, I highly recommend the Tidy Cats Breeze Litter Box System, which retails for about $30. This gets you one litter box, one scoop, one bag of pellets and four pads. You obviously have to factor in the ongoing cost of the unique pellets.

The advantage in this system is that odors are greatly reduced because the hard clay pellets do not absorb moisture. So instead, the urine drains straight down through a grid to the pad (in its own slide-out drawer), leaving the solid waste on top to be easily scooped away.

Chapter 6 - Grooming Your Birman

The sooner your Birman becomes familiar and comfortable with a grooming routine, the better. If you buy your Birman from a reputable breeder, the baby will come to you already accustomed to being combed.

Luckily with Birmans, the absence of an undercoat greatly lessens the problems of tangles and mats that other long-haired cats suffer from. A weekly brush is all that is required, but many owners choose to groom their Birman each day simply for enjoyment AND both parties' benefit!

Photo Credit: Butch & Leanne Trabuc of Kanza Katz Cattery

Discuss the cat's existing routine with the breeder, and replicate that schedule exactly. I recommend that as soon as your Birman kitten is settled, you groom them for a few minutes a day to get them used to it while they are young and they can accept it as part of their routine. At this young age, the kitten will happily turn on its back to have its belly groomed.

Also, it's always a good idea to begin and end a grooming session by concentrating on an area that feels extra good for kitty, like just below the chin. You always want your cat to associate grooming with a pleasant experience.

Birmans have a single-layer coat, which is a reason that they do not have the tendency to matt. Although they are not as hard to groom as other longhaired breeds, they do need to be brushed and occasionally bathed to keep their fur free of accumulations of oil, grit, and dander. A lot of these tasks are easily performed at home, but it's only realistic to expect to require the periodic services of a professional groomer.

All cats, including longhaired cats like the Birman, shed more in the warmer months of the year. Starting in the spring and carrying through the summer, you will likely have to increase combing sessions.

The Feline Temperament and Grooming

Professional groomers class cats in three temperamental ranges when it comes to accepting being handled and bathed:

- *Shy cats* find the grooming process frightening and must be reassured steadily and constantly. They don't tend to be aggressive, but they do try very hard to escape the whole business.
- *Compliant cats* are totally agreeable to grooming and may even enjoy it. They're not aggressive, are easy to handle, and put up no complaint whatsoever. Most Birmans fall into this category.

- *Aggressive cats* pretty much lose their minds. They can't be groomed at home, and may even require light tranquilization or actual sedation at the groomer's or vet clinic.

Clearly, the sooner a cat becomes used to being groomed, the more tolerant he'll be throughout his life.

Birmans have silky fur that is not as prone to tangling and matting as that of a Persian. Comb your Birman weekly with a shedding comb to remove loose hair and minor mats and tangles.

For grooming minor mats, small amounts of baby powder can be added. It loosens up the mats and makes them easier to comb out. Advanced mats may need the help of an experienced groomer.

Shedding combs have two sets of adjacent wire teeth with one set longer than the other. My favorites are made by Coastal Pet Safari and retail for less than $10 / £6.12.

You never want to allow any longhaired cat to develop mats that will block airflow to the skin and potentially cause itching and then infection from skin damage due to scratching.

Don't try to remove any mats that do form. Your pet's skin is very fragile and easily wounded. Minor mats can be gently teased apart with your fingers, but you must *never try to cut out a mat*. The risk of injury is too great. Under those circumstances, the services of a professional groomer are absolutely required.

Claw Clipping

Whether you are grooming your cat or a professional is undertaking the task, the first step is always to clip the cat's claws to at least bring its natural "weapons" down to a manageable level.

Get kittens used to this at a young age. It's not the clipping itself that feels weird to a kitten, it's the exposing of the nail. So when you are cuddling your new kitten on your lap, play with the paws and expose the nails (without doing any clipping) so that this feels like a normal thing to do. Kittens' claws should be clipped every week, adults every two weeks.

Birmans tend to be very compliant with all of these chores. Place the cat in your lap and pick up one front paw. Use your thumb to gently apply pressure just behind the toes so the claws will extend. The curved tips are translucent, but the vascular "quick" at the base is pink.

Be careful not to clip into this area. Not only would that cause your pet pain, but it would also result in excessive bleeding. Snip off the sharp points only and don't forget the dewclaw on the side of the foot.

I suggest following a philosophy of "less restraint." Cats don't like to feel trapped and held down. Just make sure the animal is secure in your lap. As you get more experienced with claw clipping, the chore will go quickly so the cat won't really have time to get upset.

Buy a small pair of clippers designed for use with pets. I like the ones with handles like those on pliers. The grip is better and more controlled and the price is reasonable at around $10 / £6.

The Tail Test for Bathing

If you've never given a cat a bath, and if you have no idea how your cat will react to being bathed, use the "tail test" to judge the animal's tolerance. By dragging your pet's tail through the water briefly, you will see whether he has an issue with being wet. Provided your cat doesn't go ballistic, you should be able to move forward with the bath without issue.

Use the same kind of preliminary testing if you plan on using a blow dryer. Start at the cat's tail and try working up. If the cat thinks it's being attacked by a "cat-eating monster" you'll know in a heartbeat.

Photo Credit: Anastasia Sky of Skyhaven Birmans

Actual Bathing

Always have everything you need on hand and nearby. Work with water that is lukewarm to slightly warm. Be careful not to allow water to get in the cat's ears, eyes, or nose. If possible, gently place cotton balls in the ears to ensure they stay dry.

Never pour water over the cat's face. Clean that area with a warm washcloth, but don't use soap. Cats' eyes are extremely sensitive to chemical irritation.

When the animal is thoroughly wet, there are two stages to a proper bath for a longhaired cat: degreasing and shampooing.

Find a degreasing formula specifically designed for use with pets. The substance is a paste-like gel applied and rinsed as if it were a shampoo. Degreasers cost around $15 / £9.19 for 16 ounces / 454 grams.

Pick a natural, scent-free shampoo that is hypoallergenic. Most of these products come in 16-ounce / 454-gram bottles or larger retailing for $10–$15 / £6.12–£9.19.

Work the shampoo into the fur gently. Don't scrub, as this will lead to tangling. Always over-rinse so there's no residue left in the fur, then drain all the water out of the tub and run your hands through the coat in straight motions to further remove the excess.

Swaddle the cat in a soft dry towel. Use drying strokes following the natural direction of the fur. Don't scrub!

Blow-drying is typically the home grooming deal breaker. If your cat reacts poorly to the vacuum cleaner, don't expect the blow dryer to go over well. If, however, your cat is compliant, blow in the direction of the fur while brushing in the same direction. Use the lowest setting possible. You may need help with the belly and legs.

Ear Care

Really serious ear cleaning is a job for the groomer or veterinarian. At home I don't do more than use a cotton ball dipped in warm water to swab the flap and the opening to the ear canal. Never use a cotton swab.

If you can see black, tarry debris and detect a yeasty smell, the cat likely has ear mites and will need to see the vet. The animal's ears will need a thorough cleaning and you will have to apply topical cream to kill the parasites.

Finding a Professional Groomer

If the cat isn't cooperative with home grooming, more trips to a professional will be necessary. I am a huge fan of groomers who will come to you to work with your pet at home, where the cat feels most secure and comfortable. If you do have to transport the cat to a groomer, be sure to use a sound travel crate. Never allow the cat to be loose in the car!

You can ask your breeder for a reference for a good local groomer or ask at your vet clinic. Also check the office bulletin board. Make sure that any groomer with whom you work has prior experience with Birman cats.

I suggest that you visit the grooming facility without your pet. Ask for a tour and get a clear sense of how your pet will be handled while on the premises. Pay special attention to the work areas and how they are maintained.

Specifically ask if all animals that enter the establishment are required to be current with their vaccinations. Since so many feline diseases can be communicated with nothing more than a nose tap, what precautions are taken to keep the cats strictly separated?

Grooming costs vary widely, but on average, a session should cost around $50 / £30.64.

Cat Crate

The all-important cat crate for travel and transport is not an item on which you want to scrimp. Get a quality crate that has a strong latch and fasteners. Whether you decide for a soft or hard-sided travel box, the price should still fall in a range of $25–$50 / £15–£30. This can, of course, vary by size and brand.

I also strongly recommend a crate that opens on the top as well as the side, unless you have a large Birman, this type of box is unlikely to be sturdy enough to support the weight. If you ever have a cat that is injured or sick, you can gently cradle the cat in a towel and lower him/her through the top, and then remove the cat the same way at the vet—way easier and less stressful than side loading.

Crates that have a door at the top don't cost more, and they also provide better ventilation and better visibility for the owner.

Photo Credit: Carole Morbey of Wyebrook Birman's

Chapter 7 – Feeding Your Birman

While it is certainly possible for a Birman or any other cat to require a special diet due to some sort of health condition, the vast majority thrive on the same kind of balanced and varied diet that is appropriate for any other feline companion.

Like many "facts" about cats, the idea that all cats are fussy eaters is greatly exaggerated. Just like you and I, Birman cats have foods they prefer over some others. Give me a plate full of carrots and I'll quickly pull a face of disgust rather than eat it.

Photo Credit: Christina Dyer of Snowqueen Birmans

Texture matters to a cat, as does scent. A cat will not eat what he cannot smell. If a cat has a cold or his sinuses are stopped up from seasonal allergies, the vet often prescribes giving the animal the smelliest food imaginable to stimulate its appetite. I've even had to feed mine cheap sardines that absolutely reek.

Refusing food under these circumstances isn't being "picky." It's a finally honed survival instinct that prevents these small carnivores from ingesting anything that might make them sick. By odor alone cats know what is and isn't good for them to consume. They won't touch any food that smells wrong to them or that has no scent at all.

Never try to starve a cat into eating something he doesn't want. In the first place, it won't work, but beyond that the strategy is cruel and unhealthy for the animal. If a cat suddenly refuses food he's always accepted happily, find out what's wrong, including taking the animal in for a vet checkup.

The problem could be anything from a cold to dental pain. I inherited a psychotic Himalayan from my late aunt several years ago. The breed has a lovely reputation but Ming didn't get the memo. The cranky little beast suddenly refused the one food she had loudly demanded for 12 years and I became worried even though she was an impossible member of the household.

I called the vet and took her in. When the doctor looked in Ming's mouth, the poor thing had two abscessed teeth in need of extraction. I'd be ill tempered under those circumstances, too!

Emphasize High-Quality Foods

Although it may not seem like a helpful or very specific thing to say, my honest advice is to buy the best cat food you can afford, which means those with meat as a primary ingredient. Cats are carnivores. The cheaper the food, the higher the content of grain-based fillers, thus constituting lesser quality feline nutrition.

It can also be false economy because your cat will feel hungry when he is not getting the required nutrition. It passes through their system without having much effect. So you end up spending more, by feeding more frequently!

Good quality foods have both high protein and fat content, with only a small percentage of carbohydrate required for your Birman's diet (about 5%).

The inclusion of Taurine, Niacin and Vitamin A are excellent signs of a good food as is approved by AAFCO. This stands for Association of American Feed Control Officials. This non-profit organization sets standards for pet food in the USA.

Fish, such as tuna, also contains excellent nutrients but this should only be a small part of a balanced diet.

Grow cat grass in a pot. The folic acid helps prevent anemia.

Canned pumpkin works like yogurt does for people by calming the lining of the intestines down and firming up loose stool.

I free-feed a high-protein dry food and feed canned food twice daily. There are many good brands, but I think it's better to avoid dry food that has corn meal listed in the first five ingredients. If a cat is becoming too heavy, I recommend restricting the amount of dry food, as it contains so many carbohydrates, and substituting more canned food.

Offer Wet and Dry Food

Cats thrive on a well-balanced diet that contains a mix of both wet and dry food. It is a myth that there's less litter box mess if wet foods are eliminated. Wet foods are a critical moisture source for cats and an important element of weight control.

Any cat, including a Birman, will start to pack on the pounds eating nothing but high-calorie dry food. The breed is large anyway, so it's easy to be fooled that your tubby tabby is perfectly normal. Even with a longhaired cat, you should be able to look at the body shape from above and see a slight indentation behind the ribs and just before the hips begin. If you can't see or feel this indentation, your cat is getting too fat.

It's also helpful to weigh your pet periodically and to make note of the number. Sudden weight gain or loss is an indicator of potential illness.

Just be careful to check the ingredients of any dry food, as some are excessively high in carbohydrates, which isn't doing your cat an awful lot of good, to be honest. The positive with dry food, however, is that many people believe it helps clean the teeth, leading to less dental decay. Some vets, however, will disagree, saying there is no evidence for this, but other vets do believe it helps.

Avoid All Human Food!

Like most cats, some Birmans could care less about human food, while others will beg plaintively in those funny little voices of theirs. The point is not to let them develop a taste for table scraps and treats in the first place. Any breed will become a demanding beggar if given the opportunity.

No domestic cat should be allowed to become obese. Being overweight puts your pet at risk for numerous health problems including arthritis and diabetes.

Don't court even more serious joint-related problems by allowing Fluffy to be a junk food junkie. Maybe you're no good at controlling what you eat, but you can certainly do better by your cat!

One habit you definitely don't want to start is feeding your Birman from your dinner table, or you will be nagged every time you sit down for a meal.

The same goes for feeding your kitten on the kitchen counter. If you don't want him up there don't start any encouragement and don't leave food out on the counter, as its smell will entice him to jump up there.

Schedules and Portions

I've never been much of one to carefully measure out portions for my cats unless I have an individual with a weight problem. One of my favorite domestic shorthairs was just rotund by nature. He was adorable, sweet, and packed on pounds just looking at food. He's the only cat I've ever owned who simply could not lose weight no matter what the vet and I tried.

Typically, I've always allowed my cats to free feed on dry food after they're a year old. (Free feeding just means leaving dry food out at all times.) Once they've grazed through roughly one cup (118 grams) of kibble in a day, however, I don't refill the bowl.

I'm fine giving kittens a second scoop in the afternoon because they burn up so much energy, but with adult cats I prefer their main meals to be two servings of wet food dispensed in the morning and early evening. For the average cat the servings come out to about 5.5 ounces (14.17 grams), but if you have a really big Birman with no weight issues, you can double that.

Foods That Are Toxic to Cats

Clearly, human food is not good for keeping a cat at a normal weight, but there are also many things we eat that are toxic to felines. Do not ever give your cat:

- any form of alcohol including beer
- grapes or raisins
- chocolate
- onions or chives
- raw eggs
- avocados
- yeast dough

Note that although raw eggs could be harmful for cats I have often fed my Birmans leftover scrambled eggs and eggs are also in most kitten Glop recipes. Glop is often used to supplement kittens, older cats and sick cats.

Often cats find coffee tempting, especially when it's laced with cream and sugar. Don't let your cat get away with this, or allow it anywhere near chocolate. Caffeine can be deadly to cats, and the cacao seeds used to make chocolate include methylxanthines, which are also present in soda.

These chemicals cause life-threatening symptoms including:

- excessive thirst and dehydration
- vomiting and diarrhea
- heart palpitations and arrhythmia
- seizures and tremors

Also beware of artificial sweeteners, especially those containing xylitol, which causes liver failure in cats.

Cats and the Milk Myth

As much as it's taken as a matter of "common knowledge," the idea that cats need milk or cream is really just a myth. I'm not saying your Birman *won't* lap up either dairy product, but they don't *need* the stuff, and it really isn't very good for them. Why? Well, think about it. Cow's milk is for cows. It can actually be harmful to cats. Ask anyone you know how uncomfortable it is to be lactose intolerant and you'll understand how severe the gastrointestinal upset can be. Many cats experience exactly the same thing because their bodies don't produce enough of the enzyme lactase.

Milk isn't all that great for us, either, no matter what the milk industry might have you believe. Every living mammal produces milk that is appropriate for its own young. We aren't calves any more than cats are!

As an occasional treat, there's nothing wrong with offering your cat a dish of milk, but if there are any signs of gastrointestinal upset—including an especially smelly deposit in the litter box— don't repeat the experiment.

Understanding Your Cat's Preferences

Discuss food selection with the breeder and with your vet, but also understand that cats have their likes and dislikes, which may have absolutely nothing to do with taste. You will need to learn to cater to these idiosyncrasies.

Texture preference can be hugely important in getting a cat to eat properly and well. I have one tom that loves beef pate food. Offer him chunky beef, however, and he flicks his tail and stalks away.

With Birmans, you also have to be aware of the effect of whisker stress. The breed has long, luxuriant whiskers and many don't like to reach into deep food bowls. The sensation of their whiskers dragging on the sides of the bowl is uncomfortable.

If your cat routinely drops chunks of food out on the floor to eat, whisker stress is probably the culprit. The problem can certainly affect how much the animal eats, but is easily solved with a special tray-like cat bowl. These units are somewhat expensive. They sell for $25/£16 as compared to regular food and water containers priced at $5–$10 / £3–£7, but your cat's nutritional intake will be better and you won't have messy clumps of food on the floor any more.

Photo Credit: Diane Coppola of D'Elo Birmans

Until you find a high-quality food that your cat will eat reliably and sort out all of his individual preferences, don't buy in bulk. Also, some cats happily eat the same foods daily, while others demand variety. You'll want to buy accordingly.

I completely understand the desire to have a good idea of the cost of keeping an animal, but nailing down some budgetary items like food is all but impossible. There are simply too many brands on the market. Based purely on my own experience, I would offer a conservative estimate of $75 / £45 per month on wet and dry food combined. The wet food will take up roughly a third of that budget, as it is always more expensive.

Natural or Alternative Dietary Options

Especially since the reported deaths of both dogs and cats from contaminated commercial foods, many pet owners have become interested in alternative or natural diets. This also speaks to a growing awareness of the potential dangers of chemicals and additives in highly processed products.

The most popular of the natural feeding programs for pets is a plan commonly referred to as the raw diet. I don't use it with my pets, but I am not making any recommendations for or against the approach, only offering basic information to my readers.

If you consider using this feeding program, it is imperative that you understand how much more is involved in preparing the food correctly than just putting some uncooked meat in your pet's bowl.

The idea behind the raw diet is the notion that domesticated companion animals will thrive when they eat what they would acquire for themselves if they were allowed to hunt naturally. Since cats are carnivores, this means giving them food that replicates a fresh carcass—including bones.

Most veterinarians, and many cat breeders, myself included, have heard more than enough right there. Bones create a serious choking hazard and can easily lacerate a cat's throat, stomach, and intestines. Additionally, the raw diet also increases the risk of salmonella poisoning.

The food must be handled meticulously in a spotless kitchen

with equipment reserved specifically for this purpose only. Use nothing but raw chicken and beef, *never* pork. All unused food must be discarded after 2–3 days even if it has been refrigerated, and none of the food should ever be microwaved.

Nothing I have said here is sufficient instruction to begin feeding your pets a raw diet. You must learn the precise preparation methods, acquire the correct equipment, and use only the proper food combinations to achieve the necessary balance of vitamins and minerals.

NEVER begin a raw feeding program or make any other major alteration in your pet's diet without first consulting with your veterinarian and/or breeder.

The Importance of Hydration

Be sure your Birman kitten has access to clean drinking water at all times. Wash the bowl on a daily basis to avoid a build-up of micro-organisms in the water.

I would avoid plastic food or water dishes because plastic is porous and can harbor bacteria and because of this, plastic dishes can cause "chin acne." Glass, metal or sealed pottery/china is preferable.

Wipe out the water container daily to prevent the build-up of bacteria and consider acquiring a drinking fountain to encourage better consumption in volume. Many cats won't drink from a stagnant dish.

Cat water fountains also carry the added advantage of changeable filters, which is excellent for areas with poor water quality. The units cost $30/£23 on average and from my experience last at least two years.

Chapter 8 - Your Birman Cat's Health

Birmans are marvelously healthy cats and breeders do work hard to minimize the occurrence of health problems being passed down through breeding.

A breeder who claims genetic issues have never surfaced in their cats isn't being honest. In my experience, however, when you see genetic problems with Birman cats, they are more likely to be animals from backyard breeders or worse, from kitten mills.

Please understand that I am not suggesting that backyard breeders are doing anything "bad." They have simply allowed their cat to have kittens and made those kittens available for adoption.

Photo Credit: Claire Finch of Snowwitch Birmans

The problem is that there is no control over the genetics of the pairing. It is much more likely under these circumstances for a genetic flaw to be passed on.

I would never say don't adopt a Birman cat from such a person, but would strongly recommend that you have the kitten evaluated by a veterinarian first. Also ask a lot of questions about the parents and try to get a sense of their health. Meet them if possible.

Early Spay/Neuter is becoming more and more common in the USA as a way to prevent people from becoming backyard breeders.

Spaying or Neutering

The first medical procedure your pet will require is being spayed or neutered as per the terms of the cattery's adoption agreement. (This is assuming you did acquire your cat from a recognized breeder.)

Catteries require written proof of the surgery before they will release the final registration papers. Costs vary, and there are options for having the procedure done for as little as $50 (£32.82).

Even though this is a substantial cost savings over the prices set at many clinics, I strongly suggest you find a vet in the beginning that will care for your Birman in the long term. These surgeries are the real beginning of your pet's medical records even though the baby will have likely received its initial vaccinations prior to adoption.

Spaying and neutering is usually performed for Birmans around 8–9 months of age. Since they are a slow-developing breed the extra time (compared with other breeds) helps them benefit from the hormones on the bone and joint development.

If males are altered too late in life, or if the surgery is botched, damage to the urethra makes the cat subject to painful and life-threatening bladder blockages.

Routine Health Care for Your Pet

In truth, you are the real foundation of your pet's health care program. Not only is it up to you to establish and maintain a working relationship with a qualified veterinarian, but you are also the one who will have the greatest sense of your cat's overall state of well-being due to familiarity and daily association.

Clearly in choosing a vet you want a doctor with experience treating Birmans. I am also a huge advocate of the feline-only practices that have been growing in popularity for the past 25 years. The clinics are much quieter, which keeps the cats calmer, and the vets engage in ongoing continuing education in advances specifically related to the treatment of companion felines.

Interviewing a Veterinarian

Different cat owners like different styles in their interaction with veterinarians. I want a doctor with whom I can have a detailed discussion. Information is comforting to me, especially when I am anxious and unsure. My first instinct is to calm my fears with research. I want a vet who will meet me in that place.

At the same time, however, I want a vet who will talk to me and answer my questions honestly no matter how much I may not like the answers. The animal in question is a member of my family about whom I care very much. I have to know the truth in order to make good decisions on the cat's behalf.

A highly competent vet with a lousy bedside manner when

interacting with *me* isn't someone I can work with. As for the cat, well they aren't going to enjoy going to the vet no matter what!

If you don't have a vet already, get a recommendation from the breeder, or look for local listings in the phone directory or online.

Make an initial appointment for the express purpose of interviewing the vet. Be clear about that and about the fact that you are quite willing to pay for a regular visit. Vets are busy. Don't expect one to sit down and chat with you for nothing. Treat your vet like what he or she is, a medical professional.

Go in with prepared questions. Don't overstay your welcome. Get the information you need, including a basic list of costs for procedures. Only make an appointment to go in with your cat when you are satisfied that a clinic meets your needs and those of your pet.

At that time, observe closely how the vet and the technicians work with your pet. The desired demeanor should be efficient, calm, and firm. Don't interfere with their handling of your pet unless asked. Vet techs know the best way to work with nervous, anxious cats.

Going to the Veterinarian

I'm not sure it's possible to completely say that all of the cats I have owned have enjoyed going to the vet but it's certainly possible to make the process easier and more comfortable in advance.

One of the ways I do this is to have cat carriers around the house in which they often choose to sleep and occasionally I put treats in the cat carriers, which helps my Birmans link the cat carriers with positive associations.

Vaccinations

This will also be the point in your cat's life when you decide to continue with or forego vaccinations. This is, for many pet owners, a difficult choice. I can frankly see both sides of the debate.

Vaccinating companion animals against contagious disease has, without question, been a tremendous forward step in proper pet health care for decades. This is especially true in regard to legally mandated rabies shots.

Photo Credit: Butch & Leanne Trabuc of Kanza Katz Cattery

Unfortunately, there is also credible evidence indicating that vaccinations lead to the development of tumors at the site of the injection. This is a highly individual decision that I think any cat owner should only make after careful research and in consultation with a qualified veterinarian.

When you adopt a Birman kitten from a cattery, the program of vaccinations will likely have already begun. You will have to decide whether or not you want to continue with the required boosters. The vaccinations typically given to cats include:

Combination Distemper

The combo for distemper, often referred to as FVRCP, is usually given at 8 weeks and again at 12 weeks with a booster not due until 3 years later. Some veterinarians still recommend a series of 3 shots for FVRCP—8, 12 & 16 weeks.

The intended protection includes:

- panleukopenia (FPV or feline infectious enteritis)

- rhinotracheitis (FVR, an upper respiratory/pulmonary infection)

- calicivirus (causes respiratory infections)

Some vaccines also guard against Chlamydophilia, which causes conjunctivitis.

Feline Leukemia

The leukemia vaccine is given to kittens at 2 months of age, followed by a booster a month or so later. Annual boosters are then given for life.

I cannot stress strongly enough that feline leukemia is so infectious it can be passed on by nothing more than a nose tap. You already know my belief that all cats, including Birmans, should be kept strictly indoors.

That being said, I do believe that the feline leukemia vaccine is essential for any cat that lives even part of the time outdoors. The risk of coming into contact with feral cats that are infected with the disease are simply too great.

Rabies

Most local laws require that pet owners have their animals vaccinated against rabies and that proof of this compliance can be produced. Rabies injections typically cost around $40 (£26).

Ongoing Preventive "Medicine"

The most important thing to understand about cats in regard to ongoing preventive health care is their instinctual urge to hide pain and signs of ill health. To put it bluntly, in the "real" world sick or injured animals are prey and vulnerable to attack by larger animals.

Owners must be even more vigilant about this instinct with a placid and calm breed like the Birman. It is not at all unusual for a cat to be extremely ill before the owner realizes anything is wrong.

The Importance of Daily Handling

It always strikes me as odd to say "all pets should be handled on a daily basis," since I can't keep my hands off mine, but touch and familiarity with the cat's habits and normal disposition are crucial to early detection of any abnormalities.

Never hold back from taking an animal to the vet for fear of seeming obsessive or overly concerned. No one knows your cat better than you do. If you have the sense that something is wrong, it probably is. Make an appointment!

Watch for all of the following signs of potential illness:

- Any change in weight or just the "feel" of your pet's body. Even through the coat of a Birman, you should be able to feel the ribs just under a firm pad of healthy fat.

- Pay attention to how the cat moves and jumps. Is it getting around normally? Walking easily without a limp? Pay attention to their ability to move well and without signs of discomfort.

- Look for signs of discharge from the nose or eyes. The problem could be nothing more than a respiratory infection of an allergy, but your vet still should evaluate the cat.

- Cats are very prone to infestations of ear mites. The irritation leads to scratching, which opens the door for more serious infection. Watch for ears that are hot and tender or that smell like yeast. Don't try to clean your cat's ears on your own. Make an appointment at the vet's.

- Watch for yellowed teeth, pale gums, red gums and bad breath. These are signs of plaque build-up and periodontal disease. All cats can develop cancers of the mouth and throat. Regular dental exams are not only good for their teeth, but an opportunity to screen for lesions.

- Pay attention to how the cat is breathing. Normal respiration originates in the chest, not the belly.

- While grooming or petting, feel for the presence of any type of growth or mass. Even though many such growths are benign, they should all be evaluated immediately by your vet.

- Changes in normal litter box behavior can signal the presence of painful kidney or bladder infections or even a life-threatening blockage. Don't assume an accident is an example of bad behavior. Go to the vet!

There have been enormous strides in the treatment of cats in the last two decades. Sadly, however, dog owners are still more likely to seek aggressive treatment for their pets. Don't ever make your cat a second-class citizen! Unless you are prepared to go the distance for your companion, rethink your desire to have a pet at all.

Photo Credit: Dianne Patten of Diannes Lady Paws Birmans

Worming

If you adopt a Birman kitten from a reputable cattery, the chances of the baby having intestinal parasites or "worms" is slight. You'll know, however, if worms are present. You'll see them in the litter box.

If this does occur, take the cat to the vet for a full examination. Call in advance. You will likely be asked to bring a fresh stool sample.

Turn a clean plastic bag wrong side out and put your hand inside as if the bag were a glove. Pick up the feces and fold the bag over the material, securing the bag shut. If you're a dog person, you'll recognize the maneuver from using "poop bags."

An oral deworming agent will be prescribed, with a second course of medication in 2–3 weeks to ensure all eggs have been eradicated

Giving Pills

As soon as you get your Birman make sure that you play with your kitten's mouth to get them used to the sensation so that you will be able to administer pills.

While you are cuddling your kitten, scruff him lightly (by grabbing all that loose skin around his shoulders with your left hand) and hold him upside down (his feet up) on your lap. With your right hand, play with his mouth. Use your finger to open his mouth, touch his tongue, and touch his teeth. Be playful, but make this a routine part of your cuddling sessions.

When it comes to actually administering the pill, simply scruff the cat upside down holding the pill between your thumb and index finger of the other hand. Use the middle finger of that hand to pry the mouth open, and drop the pill into the back of the cat's mouth. Gravity is working in your favor—now land it at the very back of the mouth, and the cat will never taste it but will instinctively swallow it.

Hairballs

It always amuses me when a non-cat person asks, with genuine concern, "Oh my! Did your cat throw up a hairball?" I have to restrain myself from being a smart aleck and answering, "Did the sun come up today?"

It doesn't matter what kind of cat you have, or how long their fur might be. There always comes that moment, inevitably in the dark of the night when you've been sound asleep, that the hacking starts. In theory, cats can pass hairballs rather than regurgitate them, but in 40 years with felines, I've only had one that did that.

There's no mystery attached to hairballs. They are a natural consequence of self-grooming. The only time a hairball presents a health hazard is the rare instance of a blockage, signaled by the cat's refusal to eat. If the vet takes an X-ray and finds a hairball is blocking the digestive tract, surgery may be required. Clearly the best way to help your cat with the matter of hairballs is just to brush the cat!

Potential Genetic Conditions in Birmans

Fortunately all of my Birmans have been very healthy cats and thankfully issues other breeds suffer from, such as Hip Dysplasia and PKD, are seldom ever seen in our Birmans. Nevertheless, they are possible and need explaining.

Hip Dysplasia

Hip dysplasia is caused by a defective hip socket, which causes the cat to move slowly and to be very reluctant to jump or climb. It can be quite severe, hampering movement and causing great pain, or be nothing more than a mild annoyance.

There is no way to guarantee that hip dysplasia will not be present in a line of Birmans and no breeder should ever make this claim.

Depending on the severity of the condition, it can either be controlled with pain medication, or corrective surgery may be needed.

Many people equate the hip problems associated with large dogs to large cats, but cats move differently and are more flexible. Many stories have circulated about a cat diagnosed with hip dysplasia by X-ray and yet that same cat is still able to jump to the top of a refrigerator. It just isn't as big of a quality of life issue with cats as it can be with dogs.

Hypertrophic Cardiomyopathy

Virtually any breed of cat can develop hypertrophic cardiomyopathy (HCM). The illness causes the heart muscle to thicken, reducing its capacity to function. HCM can only be detected with an echocardiogram.

As HCM spreads, fluid builds up in the lungs and blood clots form. Eventually the cat will die of heart failure. At the time of writing there is unfortunately no known cure for HCM.

HCM affects many cats, pedigreed and not. It does seem to be mainly hereditary, which is why responsible cat breeders will have the hearts of their breeding cats echoed on a regular basis (at least once a year) to try to eliminate the disease from their lines.

Ultrasound performed by a board-certified cardiologist familiar with Birmans is still the best screening device we have, although it is expensive at a cost of $600–$800 per cat. Better yet is getting a kitten not only from recently echoed parents, but who also has several screened cats behind its pedigree. Still, it's no guarantee, as heart disease is complicated. Many HCMs develop later in life when the parents (who have scanned negative) are no longer breeding.

Polycystic Kidney Disease (PKD)

Cats with Polycystic Kidney Disease (PKD) are born with cysts in their kidneys that grow as the cat ages, ultimately leading to kidney failure. The first signs of PKD appear between the ages of 3–10 years.

Symptoms can include weight loss, deterioration of the coat, poor appetite, extreme thirst, and excessive urination. Dehydration will be present with pale gums, cold breath, and ulcers in the mouth. The kidneys will also be enlarged.

PKD can only be managed, not cured. Supportive treatments like special diets, the administration of subcutaneous fluids, hormone therapy, and the use of antacids can all help your pet to enjoy a better quality of life. The Birman may live a matter of months, or do quite well for years.

Patellar Luxation

A luxating patella is a kneecap (the patella) that 'pops out of place' and is something that could afflict your Birman, especially with age, although it is more common in dogs than cats.

The term luxating means dislocated and there are four grades of patellar luxation.

You may notice the signs of limping, lameness, inability to jump as per normal or a strange skipping motion. Some Birman cats are able to live with the condition if not serious, but in other cases quick action can be preventative. Arthritis can develop, leading to pain and discomfort. Cruciate ligaments can be torn, requiring surgery. Speedy action can prevent these from occurring.

The good news is that a luxating patella can be corrected with surgery which will deepen the trochlear groove so that the patella stays in place and results in the tightening of the joint capsule and soft tissues that surround the joint, providing better stability.

After surgery your Birman cat should regain full use of its leg.

Wobbly/Shaking Kittens

Although very rare, some Birman kittens have a genetically inherited condition where the kittens wobble and tremble from head to toe from the time they start walking until 10–12 weeks. Fortunately it then disappears and the kittens walk normally, although at first sight it is alarming and distressing.

Early weaning of these kittens with a mix of baby rice and formula kitten milk is advised. Administer vitamin drops (i.e. Abidec) at a dilution of 1 part to 2 parts cooled boiled water twice a day to alleviate the condition within days.

Cat Health Network

Cats are America's most popular pet, yet they receive far less veterinary care than dogs. The goal of the CHN is to improve feline health and welfare by funding focused feline health studies. The Cat Health Network (CHN) is a collaborative effort by the American Association of Feline Practitioners (AAFP), American Veterinary Medical Foundation (AVMF), Morris

Animal Foundation (MAF), and Winn Feline Foundation (WFF).
Targeted health studies will concentrate on the areas of feline
cancer, chronic renal disease, diabetes mellitus, feline lower
urinary tract disease and pain management.

Consider donating:

http://www.morrisanimalfoundation.org/
http://www.winnfelinefoundation.org/
http://www.briafundsupporters.com/ (For FIP research).

Photo Credit: Joann Lamb of Xtasy

Chapter 9 - What to Expect As Your Birman Ages

In this chapter we take a look at the small changes that will gradually become apparent as your Birman ages. I say small because in my personal experience, changes in their senses and physical abilities are very slight and my Birmans remained quite active to the end of their lives.

Just like us, elderly cats slowly lose their ability to see, hear, smell, and taste with the same acuity they enjoyed early in life. However, cats do cope extremely well and do their best to mask these changes.

Photo Credit: Mark & Susie Harris of Mentobe Birmans

To give you an example, an elderly Himalayan cat I rescued went completely blind without me realizing until I rearranged the furniture in the living room and the poor thing started banging into chair legs. The vet confirmed that her vision was gone due to cataracts, but high blood pressure often causes blindness in elderly felines.

You may notice that older cats get thinner as their appetites diminish. This is actually tied to a decrease in their ability to smell their food, so it may be necessary to tempt a senior cat with more aromatic supper choices.

This tactic can be a two-edged sword, however. Rich foods also cause gastrointestinal upset. I opt to dribble a little fresh tuna or sardine juice on my older cats' food when they seem disinterested in eating.

This adds just enough scent to get them interested in their chow again. You can also try warming wet food just slightly to enhance the odor. If these tactics don't work, consult with your vet about safe appetite stimulants.

Physical Changes

In addition to potential changes in eating habits, older cats are leaner because they have less muscle mass. This is harder to see through a Birman's thick coat. Be sure to feel your pet's body conformation regularly. If you can feel the animal's ribs, a vet should examine the cat. Excessive weight loss is dangerous in senior cats.

Pay attention to how your cat's coat looks and help him out if he seems to need extra grooming. This includes in the more "personal" areas since arthritis may make squatting in the litter box more difficult. It's sometimes necessary to shave a longhaired cat's hindquarters to prevent soiling.

If you do have to clean your cat's "private" areas, do so with a warm washcloth and plain, clean water.

Personality Changes

Subtle changes in personality and behavior can indicate sickness or even unhappiness. If a cat with arthritis can no longer reach his favorite spot to sun, that fact can depress him the way a former athlete might look longingly at younger players on the field. Help your cat with a ramp or "stairs" so he can continue to live his life as normally as possible.

Although neither lazy nor lethargic, Birmans are mellow cats. As they age, they'll sleep for longer periods, which is just a reflection of naturally slowing down. So long as your pet is eating well, this change in behavior isn't necessarily a symptom of actual illness.

Senior cats should have regular checkups and should see the vet any time you feel uneasy about their behavior and overall demeanor. Extra vigilance is always called for, but use your judgment and your own intimate knowledge of your cat's personality and way of being in the world.

End of Life Decisions

Emotional strength is a major part of responsible pet ownership when end of life decisions are required. I have had to do this many times and always with a heavy heart, no matter how sure I was that the decision was correct. I would never presume to tell you or anyone else when it is "time." I will suggest some things, however, that might help you to make the decision.

First, take the advice of your veterinarian. I trust my vet implicitly. She knows my cats and she knows me. She doesn't lie to me or give me false hope, but she also knows that I will do whatever is necessary to support my pets' lives until they tell me it's time to go.

Yes, to a non-cat person that may sound absurd, but if I have a cat that is clearly enjoying its life but requires a treatment or a medication, euthanasia is never on the table. And no, it has not always been the wisest financial choice.

I know my cats. I know when they are in pain and are not enjoying a good quality of life. I do not believe that I have ever been responsible for causing an animal to suffer by "waiting too long." They tell me when they are done and ready to move on and I honor their wishes.

If you have not had the experience of being with a pet in those last moments, please believe what I am about to tell you. With the assistance of a kind and professional veterinarian, the process is completely dignified, fast, and painless.

In every instance my pet and I have been afforded the privacy and calm of a quiet room. I have always been given ample time to say good-bye and to hold and comfort the cat as the injection is administered.

Nothing I say can stop your pain or assuage your grief, but I hope that the knowledge that your pet will not suffer and will be treated with respect gives you some comfort when the time comes.

I also want to say that absolutely no one should ever sit in judgment on the decisions you make on behalf of your pet. I have spent large amounts of money on treatments for my cats, but I did not have family obligations that prevented me from doing so.

Whatever factors influence your decision, so long as you are motivated by kindness and a sincere desire to make the best choice for your pet that you can in the larger context of your life, no one can ask more of you.

Insurance

Thanks to advances in veterinary science our pets now receive viable and effective treatments. The estimated annual cost for your cat is $650 / £387. (This does not include emergency care, advanced procedures, or consultations with specialists.)

The growing interest in pet insurance to help defray these costs is understandable. You can buy a policy covering accidents, illness, and hereditary and chronic conditions for $25 / £16.25 per month. Benefit caps and deductibles vary by company. To get rate quotes, investigate the following companies in the United States and the UK:

United States

http://www.24PetWatch.com
http://www.ASPCAPetInsurance.com
http://www.EmbracePetInsurance.com
http://www.HealthyPawsPetInsurance.com
http://www.PetsBest.com
http://www.PetInsurance.com

United Kingdom

http://www.Animalfriends.org.uk
http://www.Healthy-pets.co.uk
http://www.Petplan.co.uk
http://www.Vetsmedicover.co.uk

Bonus Chapter 1 - Interview With Marcia Owen

I hope you have enjoyed reading this guide on Birman cats and we are not quite finished yet. This chapter is an exclusive interview which I did with Marcia Owen, an expert breeder.

Marcia, can you tell us who you are and where you are based?

I live in Northamptonshire and have been breeding Birmans since the 1980s so I feel I have come to know the Birman very well and could not envisage life without one. In these latter years I have undertaken an outcross program to help to diversify the gene pool. I have served on the Birman Cat Club committee since the late 1990s and currently maintain the club website.

My involvement in the cat world also spilled over to the GCCF Supreme Show committee for quite a considerable number of years. I think it's fair to say I have a pretty good overview of the GCCF cat world as well as showing within TICA over the last 10 years.

Just how did your interest in Birmans start?

I had bred Burmese for many years and wanted to branch out into another breed with a little more fur. I loved the gentle nature of the Birmans in contrast to the more lively nature of the Burmese.

How did you progress from owner to becoming a top breeder?

I don't class myself as a top breeder, but more of a longstanding and respected breeder who has gained that reputation through breeding for health and temperament and taking responsibility for the future of the breed and for my kittens throughout their lives.

And now you also show your cats, how did it start for you and when?

It started many years ago with the Burmese which I showed as a young teenager and naturally progressed into the Birmans when they were added to the family.

Photo Credit: Marcia Owen: On the right is Imp Gr Pr Goldlay Star Gazer (pet name Willow) and on the left is Goldlay Sugar Magnolia (pet name Sweetpea), one that I haven't shown but she has produced some stunning kittens over the years.

Can you offer any advice to others who may be wondering if they can also start showing?

Always start off with the attitude that it is a day out and if your cat wins it is a bonus. Expecting to win can lead to disillusionment. Make sure you do your research before looking at potential show cats, visit cat shows and get to know the breeders that show, and make it clear to any breeder that it is your intention to show so that you are offered a cat with show potential.

I know you are actively involved in the Birman Cat Club, can you tell our readers a little bit about the organization?

The Birman Cat Club is the nationwide breed club in the UK, founded in 1969, and it caters for all the Birman colors. The club represents the members and the breed through their membership of the GCCF and the Breed Advisory Committee. The members can look forward to participating in events organized by the club as well as contributing to its prestigious six monthly magazine.

What can a new owner expect in terms of differences between the Birman and other breeds?

There are so many breeds that it would be difficult to make comparisons, but the Birman Cat is a very gentle and affectionate breed; though needing grooming, it is much easier to look after than, say, the Persian. They are much more gentle and calmer than many of the shorthaired breeds and love to be part of your life. They are excellent cats to be around children, and are wonderful to cuddle up to in the evenings.

Are there likely to be physical differences between the Birman in the USA and in the UK?

Yes, I think the main difference is the nose; the British (GCCF) Birman does not have the Roman nose that is required by the American registries. However, the British breeders sometimes get a kitten with a Roman nose in a litter and the American breeders will get a straight nose in theirs, which can lead to useful opportunities for exchanges 'across the pond.'

Can you offer advice to people looking to buy a Birman and how much should they spend?

Do find a reputable breeder, preferably by recommendation, who is prepared to be there for you and the cat throughout the life of their pet. Make sure you visit the home of the breeder and note how happy and sociable the cat family is. You should always meet the mother, and the father if he is owned by the breeder.

Always use a breeder who registers their kittens and has them fully vaccinated before they leave and adheres to the GCCF Code of Ethics or that of the chosen registering body. You should also know exactly what the kitten eats and the type of cat litter they are used to, well in advance of your kitten leaving for their new home so that you can have your home ready for your kitten.

Always make sure, too, that if the kitten doesn't settle in your home after a reasonable space of time, the breeder will take the kitten back.

As to cost, that could be a minefield to state, as it can very quickly become out of date in a book. The best source of current prices can be advised to you by the Birman Cat Club, but remember there are regional differences driven mainly by veterinary charges for vaccinations—there can be a wide differences across the country.

Are there things that you see owners doing that frustrate you?

Hopefully by the time you have decided to let a kitten go to a family, you will have ironed out any possible frustrations, but I do like new owners to be honest with me, regarding family members in the household as well as other pets. My kittens are individual characters and I tend to match them to the right household to minimize the inevitable stresses of changing home.

How should new owners approach bringing a new kitten home, any advice and tips you can give?

Always make sure that visitors are kept to a minimum in the first week so that the kitten has time to establish itself in the house.

Make sure that you introduce the kitten to the room with the litter tray first and let them find their way around from that base.

Ensure any introductions to other pets are done in a controlled fashion and never leave them together until you are 100% sure they have made friends. Check that toilet seats are down, washing machine doors are shut and any fireplace has a fireguard in place. My kittens always go off with a whole list of dos and don'ts.

What feeding routines and types of food/supplements do you recommend?

Every breeder will have a different regime and will feed different foods. Always be guided by the breeder regarding routine and types of foods to ensure there are no upset tummies. If a kitten is fed a good quality diet there should not be a need for supplements.

Any changes to their normal diet should be phased in gradually.

What health issues should new owners be aware of?

There have been a couple of issues that have become apparent.

There can be an issue of elevated renal enzymes in Birmans but the Birman does seem to be unique in coping with them much better than other cats. If an owner has any worries in that area, then their vet should be directed to one of the large teaching universities in the UK such as Glasgow, Edinburgh or Bristol, who can give them invaluable advice.

Another emerging problem can be heart related, so again any potential new owners should seek out reputable and knowledgeable breeders to minimize the possibility of a kitten with a heart problem. The heart problem is not common at the moment and the Birman Cat Club is very active in education and fundraising for research into it.

Are there accessories that you can recommend owners buy?

A grooming kit, an activity center and plenty of toys.

Are there any final thoughts that you feel the readers of this book would benefit from?

The book should be kept to hand to dip into whenever needed. Everyone will benefit from different parts of the book at different stages of their cat's life.

Marcia Owen of Goldlay Birmans Burmese & Singapuras
http://www.goldlay-cats.co.uk

Bonus Chapter 2 - Interview With Anastasia Sky

Anastasia, could you start by introducing yourself and telling us where you live?

My name is Anastasia Sky and I live in Dundas, Ontario, Canada. I am a physician by profession and I also own a cattery called Skyhaven Birmans. I have been breeding Birman cats since 2005.

I gather you have just achieved a very important accomplishment in the Birman cat world, perhaps you could tell us what just happened?

This year, our Birman cat GC, BW, RW Skyhaven Leopold Mozart became CFA's Best of Breed Birman 2015. This means he is the highest scoring Birman cat in the world in CFA in 2015 from all Birmans in Championship worldwide.

Also this year Skyhaven Birmans has been awarded a CFA

Distinguished Merit award for our Birman female GC Skyhaven Jezebelle, DM. Jezebelle is a homegrown Grand Champion whose five children from her first two litters became Grand Champions, and this earned her the DM title.

Skyhaven Birmans granded eight Birman cats in CFA during the 2014–2015 show season.

This is also the third year in a row that Skyhaven Birmans have had CFA Regional Winners.

Now that is quite a success story. Going back to the beginning, how did you first come into contact with the Birman cat?

In 2005 I purchased my first Birman female cat in Ohio, USA, with the intention of owning a beautiful and loving pet.

How did you go from being an owner to getting into breeding?

I bred my first Birman female cat, which I had purchased in 2005, to a male Birman stud in New York, USA. This breeding produced a beautiful Lilac Point male kitten named Skyhaven Dewey in the first litter. Dewey became a CFA Grand Champion and this was my first CFA Grand. Dewey has a splendid personality which compliments his beauty. It was these traits, plus Dewey's show achievement, that attracted me to breeding Birmans.

What makes people enquire about a Birman over another breed of cat?

In my experience people who inquire about Birmans are looking for two things: a very loyal and friendly family pet which is also strikingly beautiful. Pet buyers are attracted to the deep blue eyes, white gloves and laces, and their loving nature most of all.

Do you think the breed is becoming more popular, less popular or staying the same?

My impression is that locally in our area Birmans are becoming more popular than ever. I can't speculate, however, as to how this compares with the popularity of other cat breeds worldwide.

What do you look for in a prospective owner?

In a prospective owner I look for the ability and commitment to take care of a cat very well, and also the love a family can offer a Birman pet.

And the show side of things, how did that start for you?

I began showing Birmans in CFA in 2005—my very first Birman cat. Showing is a big commitment and requires discipline, enthusiasm, and endurance on the part of the person who is showing the cats.

How would an owner know they have a show-quality cat and how would they start off?

Usually the breeder who sells a cat might inform their buyer if their kitten/cat is show quality. The head-type, ear-set, expression, body, coat, marking symmetry, and temperament all come into play. If someone would like to show a Birman cat rather than just own a pet, a "Show Sales Contract" might be possible to arrange with their breeder if both parties agree.

Showing would require some mentorship instruction from the breeder or someone else who has good showing experience.

Is showing very expensive and why do you think people like to do it?

Showing can be quite expensive. The cost depends on how many shows are attended and the frequency of showing. People enjoy the art of preparation for a show, the grooming prior and in the show hall itself, and the recognition from peers and onlookers appreciating their treasured Birman. There is also the thrill of achievement and the joy of exhibiting one's creative efforts.

Can you give away any of your secrets?!

Excellent nutrition, love, and thoughtful choices when selecting breeding pairs are three important keys to happy and healthy Birmans.

What do judges look for in a winner?

Good temperament, a proper Birman head-type (which includes a wide ear-set, a Roman nose and a strong chin), solid body structure, and a strong blue eye color are all features that make a winner.

That special sweet expression is also a plus.

What do you think makes the Birman cat special to you?

The Birman personality makes this breed the most special for me.

Do you have any feeding advice or brands that you prefer?

I recommend that Birmans eat as much grain-free moist foods as possible. I recommend higher-end foods rather than grocery store varieties, and rotating cat food varieties is good to ensure cats don't lose interest in their food. It is important to give Birman cats moist food daily and not only kibble.

What sort of health issues should owners be on the lookout for?

A trusted veterinarian will set up a good check-up schedule for a Birman and it is important to always keep up with these recommendations.

Staying away from poisonous plants such as lilies and other poisonous plants is important.

Birman cats cannot metabolize Ketamine anesthetic, something that some veterinarians may not know. Ketamine can kill Birmans and should never be used. Data about the dangers of Ketamine in Birmans has not been widely reported in scientific literature, but it is true. I advise my pet buyers to ensure Ketamine is never used for their Birman.

Thank you Anastasia for sharing your story and experiences.

Anastasia Sky
Skyhaven Birmans
Canada
http://www.skyhavenbirmans.com/

Bonus Chapter 3 - Interview with Heather Reynolds

Heather, thanks for doing this interview, can you tell us who you are and where you are based?

My name is Heather Reynolds and I am based in Guelph, Ontario, Canada. I have worked for many years in healthcare with a focus on clinical therapeutic nutrition and food safety in the hospital setting.

When did you first become a Birman owner and did you expect to become a breeder at that point?

I purchased an adult blue point Birman as a pet in 2005. I have always had a keen interest in genetics and animal husbandry, but prior to this time raising my family and working at a challenging career in a large city about an hour from home required most of my time and resources. When the children were older and more independent, I felt the timing was right to pursue a hobby with pedigree cats. We had previously owned other breeds of cats and dogs as pets, but I approached my new hobby by doing considerable research and subsequently found the Birman and decided that I would like to pursue breeding my own.

How have you found being a Birman breeder—is it a lot harder than might be obvious to people?

When I look back at those early years I can't imagine what I would have done without the mentorship of the experienced Birman breeders I met along the way. As prepared as I thought my research had made me, nothing beats first hand, trial by fire experience and advice from a successful longtime breeder. It is a hobby of extremes...there is tremendous satisfaction and joy in producing healthy, happy, beautiful kittens that either become a treasured family member with a pet family or that shine in the show hall. But there are some very dark and scary times when you have to make very difficult decisions. Having a mentor when you start breeding and a network of friends is, in my opinion, what makes the difference in whether a person stays in the hobby. And the money of course...there is a breeder saying that if you are making money breeding cats you are not doing it right. We laugh about it, but in all seriousness you have to have a passion to combine art and science in breeding, because by doing it well you will likely spend far more than you will ever recoup.

You have gone on to show your cats, how did that start?

I feel that showing is a crucial component in a good breeding program. It is the method by which we get unbiased expert feedback on how well our breeding decisions are moving us toward the written standard of what makes a Birman unique among the breeds.

What achievements have you accomplished?

That's hard to quantify because I don't show as much yet as I'd like to. Perhaps when I retire I will be able to travel more. I'm pleased that our show cats tend to be recognized by judges as being worthy of becoming CFA Grand Champions fairly quickly and hope that in the future I will have the time to show them beyond that. I guess the best way to answer is that we show in a highly competitive region and our Birmans hold their own in the show hall against many beautiful Birmans that go on to higher awards.

I'm sure a lot of readers think there's lots of mystery behind these cat shows, but how did it start for you and when?

I went to my first cat show with another breeder whom I had purchased my first show/breeder kitten from. She ingrained the need to network and have your breeding evaluated to avoid 'cattery blindness': the tendency for one to become blind to kittens' faults because of emotional attachment to them.

Is it an impossible dream or can anybody start to show?

The best way to get started showing is to find a breeder who produces show cats and talk to them about learning to show a neutered Birman. There are often very nice show-quality kittens that a breeder will place as pets because he or she cannot keep them as breeding cats. This is a great way to meet other breeders and learn the nuances of the breed standard, as well as the logistics and mechanics of showing.

What really determines success at a cat show?

There is a lot of talk of politics, but honestly I have not experienced much of that. Different judges do appreciate different looks and styles within the written standard. I think many people use politics as an excuse for not doing as well as they had hoped...but we need to remember that the judges look at the cats as they appear TODAY and slight changes in coat or condition for the better or worse affect which cats the judges select.

Obviously the cat needs to meet the standard, but as you gain experience you will start to be able to identify those additional characteristics that make a successful show Birman stand out.

And they have to have the temperament for showing—a cat that enjoys the attention and is relaxed and happy being shown is a joy to present to a judge.

Why do you think people should choose the Birman breed over another breed of cat?

I enjoy the Birmans' wonderful social temperament. They love having friends and company—very few are truly solitary. Birmans are gregarious and get on well with other friendly animals, they enjoy gentle children and are true and loyal companions. I love how mine all run to greet me as soon as they hear me pull in the driveway after work. Birmans make fantastic companions without the drawbacks of a dog.

What advice would you give to people who are looking to buy a Birman cat?

People looking to purchase a Birman need to not only research the breed but also the breeder. Certainly use the Internet to find names of breeders, but also consider that you will have this pet for a long time and traveling to meet and purchase from a breeder who produces great kittens and will support you through the years is a relatively small investment. A Birman breeder should be registered with one of the major associations and register the litter. Show success and flashy webpages do not always translate into healthy breeding practices that produce top-quality, well socialized kittens. It is very important to ask questions about the health of the parents and previous breedings.

Nothing beats visiting the cattery in person and seeing firsthand the care and health of the cats that live there. Kittens should be curious and have clear, clean eyes and noses as well as back ends. The environment should be clean and the kittens should be accustomed to interacting with people. In my opinion, caging kittens for the duration of their kittenhood affects their temperament. There are times when caging can be appropriate, such as confining a queen just prior to and just post birth. Also briefly if a litter of kittens is challenged learning to consistently use the litterbox. Or when they require medical care. It is not wise to allow kittens to run with the group of adult cats. But I have found the most confident and friendly temperaments are formed when kittens are allowed to play and grow up in a well-visited, baby-proofed room in a home.

A breeder should be proud to offer you information about the background of their breeding lines. They will be happy to discuss testing and veterinary care that they have on their breeding cats.

Finally, there should be a written contract that stipulates what sort of health and genetic guarantee are offered by the breeder. It will often also outline the expectations the breeder has for the kitten's new home. This should include an obligation to spay or neuter if the kitten isn't already altered. Often there is a rehoming clause that states that the kitten is to be returned if it is no longer wanted and that it will not be placed in a shelter, rescue or sold to a lab.

Finally, remember that the breeder is who you may be dealing with if things go awry or if you need support down the road...a breeder that you feel you could call up a few years from now for advice or support and that will remain interested in your kitten's well-being long after the check is cashed is worth the travel.

Do you think there is a minimum amount, realistically, that people should be spending?

In Canada I would be suspicious if I saw kittens listed for sale under $750 for a 14–20-week-old. Given the cost of ensuring the parents are appropriate to breed and raising a litter properly, that would barely cover a breeder's expenses. On occasion there may be an individual kitten that was retained until they were older or that may have a disclosed defect that might be offered at a discount. For example, I would not place a kitten that I was not confident in, and from time to time I have had one that just didn't grow as the others in their litter did. I have kept these kittens and investigated why they were slow to grow. When they were placed at 6 or 7 months they were discounted and the owners were advised of why I had kept them so long. They all grew up to be healthy adults, but we didn't know that would be the case when they were younger.

What would you say are common mistakes that you have seen Birman owners make?

On occasion a few new pet owners have underestimated how much their young Birman kitten depends on them emotionally. Kittens have difficulty being left all alone for long periods of time or being separated from their owners during the night. Sometimes people don't follow our suggestion of keeping a new kitten confined in a small room when they are not home. A large space can be overwhelming for a new kitten and it may hide or have difficulty remembering where its litter box is.

Grooming is important, can you offer any tips, advice and perhaps some accessories that you wouldn't be without?

Ideally many Birmans are bred to have an almost maintenance-free coat. However, there are ones that require some more frequent combing to prevent matting, especially during periods of high shedding such as the spring molt. A good steel comb that can get down to the skin without tearing the coat is the most important tool. Combing once a week during the winter and summer is usually sufficient, and most Birmans really enjoy this. During the spring, a once a day comb will help prevent tiny tangles from becoming mats. Important to remember is that if you should ever encounter a mat that can't be combed out— always work the comb between the mat and the skin and then gently snip the hairs on the comb side with a pair of small scissors. Cat skin is very elastic and difficult to see and can be easily cut if you don't protect it by using a comb between the scissors and the skin.

Are there health issues new owners should be aware of?

Heart disease appears to be on the rise around the world. Ask your breeder about his or her experience with their cats. Many breeders are having heart screening done on breeding cats, although that isn't necessarily a guarantee that the cats won't develop it later in life. Projects are currently underway to identify genetic markers specific to the type of cardiomyopathies being observed in Birmans. At this time there has not yet been a breed-specific DNA test validated, however an honest and knowledgeable breeder should be able to discuss the health history of the bloodlines they have been working with and what measures they have put in place to mitigate the risks of producing Birmans with cardiomyopathies.

Are there any final thoughts that you want to share?

Your new Birman kitten is the culmination of generations of care and effort of many breeders. Treasure them as a cherished member of your family and they will repay you tenfold in love, companionship and loyalty.

Thanks so much Heather for sharing your expertise.

Heather Reynolds of Gryphonwood Birmans
https://sites.google.com/site/gryphonwoodbirmans/

Useful Birman Websites

The Cat Fanciers' Association, Inc.
http://www.cfainc.org

The International Cat Association
http://www.tica.org

The American Cat Fanciers' Association (ACFA).
http://www.acfacat.com/

National Birman Fanciers (CFA)
http://www.nationalbirmanfanciers.com

Sacred Cat of Burma Fanciers Cat Club
http://www.scbf.com/

Birman Cat Club of Canberra
http://www.actbirmanclub.com.au

Birman Cat Club of New Zealand
http://www.birmancatclub.co.nz

The Birman Cat Club UK
http://www.birmancatclub.co.uk

North American Birman Fanciers
http://www.birman.org

Birman Welfare and Rescue
http://www.birmanrescue.co.uk

Birmans Online
http://www.birmanbreeder.com

Frequently Asked Cat Behavior Questions

In this section we cover general cat behavior. The answers in this section will apply not only to your Birman, but to all breeds of cats.

Why does a cat "knead"?

When a kitten is nursing, it typically kneads its paws against its mother, either as a sign of contentment or to encourage the milk flow. When the cat matures, it kneads to show its contentment and pleasure.

Why does your cat wash your hair or face?

Before it can even see, a kitten experiences its mother licking and washing. Grooming is a demonstration of love and caring, so your cat is showing you his acceptance and caring of you as a fellow feline.

Why does a cat go to the visitor who doesn't like cats?

When one cat is threatening another, it stares boldly, sometimes hisses, and frequently moves in toward the other cat. Usually, the person who doesn't like cats avoids looking at it, doesn't talk to it, and sits quietly, hoping to be ignored by the cat. The cat, therefore, sees the person's behavior as "cat-friendly" and practically inviting.

Why does your cat push its head against you?

This is called "head butts" and is a cat's way of showing affection. Some cats will turn their head, and push it against a human (or another cat).

Why does your cat rub up against you?

Cats have scent glands along the tail, on each side of their head, on their lips, base of their tail, chin, near their sex organs, and between their front paws. They use these glands to scent mark their territory. When the cat rubs you, he is marking you with his scent, claiming you as "his." Cats rub up against furniture or doorways for the same reason—to mark the item as "his." (Urine spraying is also a territorial marking, by the way.)

Why does a cat scratch outside the litter box, instead of inside it?

The cat has probably had several unpleasant experiences of getting his feet soggy or dirty—make sure the litter box is cleaned out frequently.

Why does a cat sometimes scratch the floor as though he is trying to bury his food dish?

It may be a holdover of the wild trait of burying food for later. Or, it may be that he is trying to tell you that the food is not to his liking.

Why does a cat attack humans' ankles?

Kitten play always involves mock battles, with surprise attacks, pounces, and leaps. The kitty is basically trying to play, as he would with another cat. Direct him to less painful game play—chasing balls, cords, and so on.

Why does your cat turn his/her back on you after a scolding, or if you've been gone for a while?

Typically, a person's body language when reprimanding a pet

includes staring or other overtly "aggressive" behavior. The cat usually responds in a submissive fashion. In a sense, it is telling you he has surrendered to you, as a fellow cat, and is discouraging attack.

Why does your cat bring you dead or dying creatures?

There are at least four differing theories on this behavior:

- Your cat is bringing you a present, in appreciation for you feeding it or as a sign of affection.
- Your cat realizes you are a totally incompetent mouser and is trying to educate you.
- The cat is bringing her prey home to where it is safe, where she usually eats.
- The cat is simply trying to make sure you have fresh food.

Why does a cat play with its prey?

Cats are attracted by movement, so if a stalked prey keeps moving, the cat's desire to attack continues to be stimulated. If the cat gets very excited over the stalking/killing, he may continue to play with the prey after it is dead.

Why do cats roll over on their backs?

Cats roll over on their backs for a variety of reasons: if your cat flops down in front of you and rolls over on his back for a belly rub, it's a sign of his complete trust in you that you won't ever hurt him. Other times, he wants to play. If the cat is female and in heat, it's a form of foreplay. It's also a part of their social standing. Domesticated cats don't display this as much as wild ones do.

Why do some cats go crazy over catnip, but others ignore it?

The response to catnip is the result of a gene in the cat; if the cat doesn't have the gene, it cannot physically react to catnip. Some cats will react to catnip by rolling around on the floor in delight, others will just quickly eat it up and wander off, while others will ignore it completely.

Why does a cat sometimes "sneer" when smelling something?

When a cat curls back its upper lip and looks like it's sneering, it has just discovered an interesting, usually intense odor and is smelling it more deeply. Called "flehming," it is drawing the odors into an organ (Jacobson's organ) in the roof of its mouth.

Why do some cats insist on drinking from a dripping faucet/tap?

Cats—like most other animals—prefer their food and water fresh, and running water is most appealing for that reason. Also, the motion of water coming out of a faucet is probably appealing to their sense of hearing and sight.

Why does a cat hide when it is sick or dying?

Instinct tells a cat to hide where a predator can't find them. When a cat is ill, it may think it is being stalked—so it hides.

Why does a cat spend so much time grooming?

Besides the obvious purpose of hygiene and the social aspects, grooming helps cats cope with confrontation or embarrassment (you may have noticed that if a cat accidentally falls off a chair, the first thing he does is nonchalantly wash himself, as though he intended to get down in the first place).

Why does a cat scratch the furniture or a scratching post?

While some people think a cat scratches to sharpen its claws, that is probably inaccurate. There are typically two reasons for scratching: the cat is marking its territory (cats have sweat glands between their paw pads, and scratching leaves their scent on the clawed object); or, the cat is "filing down" its nails and removing the outer layer.

Why does a cat suddenly bite or hiss at a person after it's been petted for a while?

If a person persists in touching a sensitive area (such as the cat's tail, ears, or belly), the cat might give a gentle nip as a way of staying "stop." Or, some cats can tolerate pleasurable stroking only for short periods of time; again, he may communicate "stop it" with a nip or cuff of his paw.

Why do some cats insist on tipping over their water dish, or taking food out of the dish and dropping it on the floor to eat?

Most cats do not like to eat or drink out of bowls if the sides touch their whiskers. Also, if a bowl is too deep, the cat may take the food out for convenience. A wider, shallower bowl will probably eliminate this behavior.

Why do cats chew on plants?

It could be that the grass helps the cat get rid of fur swallowed while grooming, or that grass provides fiber or vitamins and minerals not found in meat. Some plants are poisonous to a cat; others are okay for nibbling.

Glossary

Ailurophile - A lover of cats.

Ailurophobe - One who fears and/or hates cats.

Allergen - The primary allergen produced by cats to which sensitive individuals react is the protein Fel d 1 produced by the animal's sebaceous and salivary glands. Fel d 1 is especially spread in the environment by dried flakes of saliva on the fur from grooming.

Allergy - An individual exhibiting a high degree of sensitivity to a known irritant, as in the Fel d 1 in cats. The symptoms of the allergic reaction may include sneezing, itching and watering of the eyes, and skin rashes.

Alter - A term used in reference to the surgical procedures that render companion animals incapable of reproduction, i.e. neutering or spaying.

Bloodline - A bloodline establishes an animal's pedigree by supplying a verifiable line of descent. Catteries carefully cultivate their animals' bloodlines in an effort to produce the highest possible exemplars of the given breed.

Breed Standard - Breed clubs and official feline organizations like The International Cat Association (TICA) formulate standards of excellence for the breed to be used as a basis for evaluating the quality of the animals for breeding and showing purposes.

Breed - An animal is said to belong to a particular breed when it shares specifically defined physical characteristics derived from a common ancestry that "breed true" or are reliably passed on to subsequent generations.

Breeder - A breeder is an individual who works to produce superior examples of a given breed of cat (or other animal) through the carefully selected pairing of dams and sires. The principle purpose of breeding is to both maintain and improve the genetic quality of the breed in question.

Breeding - Breeding refers to the pairing of dams and sires in controlled reproductive programs for the express purpose of producing high-quality offspring.

Breeding Program - A breeding program is a planned mating of carefully chosen dams and sires to cultivate ideal examples of a given breed.

Breeding Quality - An animal's breed quality describes the degree to which an individual conforms to the breed standard for subsequent purposes of show or participation in a breeding program.

Breed True - When male and female cats of a given breed mate and produce offspring that possess the same traits, all conforming to the recognized standard for the breed, the line is said to "breed true."

Carpal Pads - A cat's carpal pads are located on the front legs at the region roughly correlating with the human wrist. Their purpose is to provide greater traction for the animal while walking.

Castrate - The surgical removal of a male cat's testicles to render him incapable of impregnating females.

Caterwaul - A shrill and discordant feline vocalization.

Cat Fancy - The "cat fancy" is an aggregate term to define all of the groups, associations, and clubs as well as their members that exist for the purpose of breeding and showing cats.

Catnip - Cat nip (Nepeta cataria) is a perennial herb containing high levels of an aromatic oil to which cats are strongly attracted. In response to exposure to "nip," cats display a kind of intoxication similar to what humans experience when they are "stoned." A cat must be older than 8–9 months of age to respond to catnip, and some individuals are completely immune to the herb's effects.

Cattery - A cattery is a facility where cats are kept for the purpose of breeding to promulgate a specific breed and bloodline.

Certified Pedigree - A certified pedigree is one that has been officially issued by a feline registering association.

Clowder - The collective term "cloudier" refers to an assemblage or group of cats.

Coat - The overall term used in reference to a cat's fur.

Crate - A crate is a container used for the safe transport or temporary confinement of cats and other small companion animals.

Crepuscular - The correct term to describe the times at which cats are most active, dawn and dusk. Contrary to popular perception, cats are not nocturnal.

Crossbred - When a dam and sire of different breeds produce offspring, the kittens are said to be crossbred.

Dam - In a breeding pair of cats, the female is the dam. Also called a queen.

Dander - Dander is often responsible for the allergic reaction some sensitive people display in the presence of cats. The small scales are shed by the animal's hair and skin, and contain the Fel d 1 protein from the animal's saliva transferred during self-grooming.

Declawing - Declawing is a surgical procedure to amputate the last digit of a cat's feet for the purpose of removing its claws. The operation is illegal in Europe, and also in many parts of the United States. Declawing is highly controversial and generally considered to be inhumane and cruel.

Desex - Desexing is the alteration of an animal by neutering or spaying to render the individual incapable of reproduction.

Domesticated - Animals that live and/or work tamely with humans whether by training or choice.

Ear Mites - Ear mites are microscopic parasites that cause extreme itching and discomfort by feeding on the lining of a cat's ear canal. Their presence generates a strong, foul odor and causes a build-up of black, tarry debris.

Entire - A cat is said to be "entire" when the individual is in possession of its complete reproductive system.

Exhibitor - An individual who participates in an organized cat show competitively with his or her animal or animals.

Fel d 1 - The Fel d 1 protein is produced by a cat's sebaceous glands and is also present in the animal's saliva. This is the substance that triggers an adverse allergic reaction in some sensitive people.

Feline - Felines are members of the family *Felidae*, which includes lions, tigers, jaguars, and both wild and domestic cats.

Fleas - Fleas are wingless, bloodsucking insects in the order *Siphonaptera* that feed off warm-blooded animals causing scratching and skin irritation, and in severe cases, anemia.

Flehmening/Flehmen Reaction - The Flehmen Reaction is a facial gesture in cats often mistaken for a grimace. When a cat partially opens its mouth and curls back its upper lip, the animal is drawing air over two special openings in the roof of the mouth just behind the front teeth. These second "nostrils" allow a cat to "taste" what it is smelling.

Gene pool - In any population of organisms, the "gene pool" is the group's collective genetic information.

Genes - Genes are the distinct hereditary units consisting of a DNA sequence that occupies a specific location on a chromosome. Genes determine the particular physical characteristics of an organism.

Genetic - Any trait, characteristic, tendency, or condition that is inherited is said to be genetic in nature.

Genetically Linked Defects - Specific health conditions or other perceived flaws that are passed from one generation to the next are considered to be genetically linked defects.

Genetics - Genetics is the scientific study of heredity.

Genotype - The genetic makeup of an organism or a group of organisms is called the genotype.

Grooming - The necessary procedures to care for the coat of a feline are called grooming and typically include brushing, combing, trimming, or washing.

Heat - When a female mammal such as a cat enters her seasonal estrus cycle the phase is colloquially referred to as "going into heat."

Hereditary - Characteristics, traits, diseases, or conditions genetically transmitted from parent to offspring are said to be hereditary.

Histamine - A physiologically active amine released by mast cells in plant and animal tissue as part of an allergic reaction.

Hock - The anatomical term for that part of a cat's hind leg that is the rough equivalent of the human ankle.

Household Pet - Unlike dog shows, cat shows have a division for "household pets," which are non-pedigreed individuals. This competition is extremely popular with young people and a starting ground for many new enthusiasts in the cat fancy.

Housetraining - The process of teaching an animal to live cleanly in a house using a box of sand or gavel litter for urination and defecation is called "housebreaking."

Immunization - Immunizations, also called inoculations or vaccinations, are injections intended to create immunity against disease.

Innate - Qualities, traits, and tendencies that are present at birth and therefore inborn are said to be innate.

Inbreeding - The mating of two closely-related cats is said to be inbreeding, and is typically the cause of genetic defects.

Instinct - Inborn patterns of behavior in a species that are triggered by specific environmental stimuli are called "instincts."

Intact - Animals that have not been spayed or neutered and that are in possession of their complete reproductive system are said to be intact.

Jacobsen's Organ - This is a highly specialized organ in the roof of a cat's mouth. Two extra "nostrils" located just behind the upper front teeth allow the cat to "taste" a scent when air passes over the openings.

Kindle - A "kindle" is a collective term for a group of cats, but in this instance refers specifically to kittens.

Kitten - A kitten is a cat of less than 6 months of age.

Lactation - The formation and secretion of milk by the mammary glands for the nourishment of young mammals.

Litter - Felines give birth to 3–4 kittens on average, with 6–10 possible. These multiple offspring groups are referred to as litters.

Litter Box - A litter box is a container holding sand or clay that allows a cat to live cleanly in the house by providing the animal with an acceptable place to urinate and defecate.

Longhaired - Any breed of cats, like a Persian, that have a coat made up of varying lengths of long hair. These same animals usually also display prominent neck ruffs and plumed tails.

Mites - Tiny parasites from the order *Acarina* are called mites.

They infest both plants and animals, and are often present in the ear canals of domestic cats.

Muzzle - That part of the head and face of a cat that projects forward. This region includes the mouth, nose, and jaws, and may also be referred to as the snout.

Neuter - A term used to describe the surgery for castrating a male cat to prevent him from impregnating a female.

Nictitating Membrane - The dictating membrane is the transparent inner or "third" eyelid on cats that protects and moistens the eye.

Nocturnal - Animals that are nocturnal are most active at night. This term is used in error with cats, as these creatures are most active at dusk and dawn and are therefore crepuscular.

Odd-Eyed - In odd-eyed cats, each eye is a different color.

Papers - The colloquial term for the official documentation of a cat's pedigree and registration is "papers."

Pedigree - A pedigree is the written verifiable ancestry of a cat of a particular breed spanning three or more generations.

Pet Quality - A pet-quality pedigreed cat is one that fails to sufficiently conform to the standard for the breed to be used in a breeding program or to be exhibited for competition.

Queen - Queens are intact female cats in possession of their complete reproductive system.

Quick - The "quick" of a cat's claw is the vascular portion at the base that will bleed profusely if accidentally clipped.

Rabies - Rabies is a highly infectious viral disease fatal in warm-blooded animals. It is transmitted by the bite of an infected animal and attacks the victim's central nervous system.

Registered Cat - A registered cat is one that has been documented via a recognized feline association in regard to its breed and pedigree.

Registered Name - A cat's registered name is the name used to verify its breed and pedigree. Names are typically long, and made up of a combination of the names of the cat's sire and dam.

Scratching Post - Any structure covered in carpet or rope and designed to be used by a cat to sharpen and clean its claws without being destructive to household furnishings is referred to as a scratching "post."

Show - Cat shows are organized exhibitions where cats are judged competitively for the degree to which they conform to accepted breed standards.

Show Quality – Show-quality cats in any breed are those that conform sufficiently to the recognized standard for their type to be included in breeding programs and to be exhibited in competitions.

Sire - In a breeding pair of cats, the male is referred to as the sire.

Spay - Spaying is the surgical procedure whereby a female cat's ovaries are removed, rendering her incapable of reproduction.

Spray - Spraying is a territorial behavior typically seen in male cats. Using a stream of pungent urine, the cat marks its territory, often as part of a competition with other males for the attention of a female.

Stud - Studs are male cats that are intact and are therefore qualified to participate in a breeding program.

Subcutaneous - Subcutaneous means just below the skin, and typically refers to an injection or to the administration of supplemental fluids in cats with kidney deficiencies.

Tapetum Lucidum - The tapetum lucidum is the interior portion of a cat's eye. The structure is highly reflective and helps the cat to see effectively in low light. Cats cannot, however, see in total darkness.

Vaccine - Vaccines are dead or weakened preparations of a bacterium, virus, or other pathogen. They are injected into an individual for the purpose of stimulating the production of antibodies to cultivate immunity against disease.

Wean - Weaning is the point in a kitten's development when it gradually gives up its mother's milk as its primary means of nutrition and begins to take solid foods.

Whisker Break - The whisker break on a cat is an indentation on the upper jaw.

Whisker Pad - The thickened or fatty pads on either side of a cat's face holding rows of sensory whiskers.

Whole - A cat of either gender that is in possession of its reproductive system is said to be whole.

Index

Lightning Source UK Ltd.
Milton Keynes UK
UKHW050701100322
399803UK00014B/555